T0047283

Editor: Sasha Lilley

Spectre is a series of penetrating and indispensable works of, and about, radical political economy. Spectre lays bare the dark underbelly of politics and economics, publishing outstanding and contrarian perspectives on the maelstrom of capital—and emancipatory alternatives—in crisis. The companion Spectre Classics imprint unearths essential works of radical history, political economy, theory and practice, to illuminate the present with brilliant, yet unjustly neglected, ideas from the past.

Spectre

Greg Albo, Sam Gindin, and Leo Panitch, *In and Out of Crisis: The Global Financial Meltdown and Left Alternatives*

David McNally, *Global Slump: The Economics and Politics of Crisis and Resistance*

Sasha Lilley, *Capital and Its Discontents: Conversations with Radical Thinkers in a Time of Tumult*

Sasha Lilley, David McNally, Eddie Yuen, and James Davis, *Catastrophism: The Apocalyptic Politics of Collapse and Rebirth*

Peter Linebaugh, *Stop, Thief! The Commons, Enclosures, and Resistance*

Peter Linebaugh, *The Incomplete, True, Authentic, and Wonderful History of May Day*

Richard A. Walker, *Pictures of a Gone City: Tech and the Dark Side of Prosperity in the San Francisco Bay Area*

Spectre Classics

E.P. Thompson, *William Morris: Romantic to Revolutionary*

Victor Serge, *Men in Prison*

Victor Serge, *Birth of Our Power*

Patriarchy of the Wage

Notes on Marx, Gender, and Feminism

Silvia Federici

BTL

SPECTRE

PM

Patriarchy of the Wage: Notes on Marx, Gender, and Feminism
Silvia Federici
© 2021 PM Press.

ISBN: 978-1-62963-799-0 (paperback)
ISBN: 978-1-62963-858-4 (hardcover)
ISBN: 978-1-62963-809-6 (ebook)

Library of Congress Control Number: 2019946095

Cover by John Yates / www.stealworks.com
Interior design by briandesign

10 9 8 7 6 5 4 3 2 1

PM Press
PO Box 23912
Oakland, CA 94623
www.pmpress.org

Autonomedia
PO Box 568 Williamsburg Station
Brooklyn, NY 11211-0568 USA
info@autonomedia.org
www.autonomedia.org

This edition first published in Canada in 2021 by Between the Lines
401 Richmond Street West, Studio 281, Toronto, Ontario, M5V 3A8,
Canada
1-800-718-7201
www.btlbooks.com

ISBN: 978-1-77113-497-2
Canadian Cataloguing in Publication information available from
Library and Archives Canada
Printed in the USA

Contents

Introduction

The celebrations of the 150th anniversary of Marx's *Capital* have shown the lasting power of Marx's political theory, bringing together scholars who have dedicated their lives to studying his work, as well as younger activists who are drawn to it by what appears to be a prolonged capitalist crisis, signaled by the near collapse of the world financial system in 2008, the diminishing growth rate, and the dire predictions concerning the economic consequences of the Covid epidemic, which some anticipate will be harsher than the Great Depression of 1929.

Among feminists as well there has been a revival of interest in Marx, partly because of the intensifying crisis of social reproduction and partly as a reaction against past postmodern trends, which, by their refusal of broad social theories and their stress on cultural diversity, have curtailed our ability as feminists to provide a critique of capitalist relations.

What the feminist return to Marx has demonstrated is that his methodology and critique of capitalism remain a necessary foundation for an analysis of women's exploitation in capitalist society. Indeed, it is difficult, even after the changes that capitalism has undergone since Marx's time, to think of contemporary social reality without turning to *Capital* or the *Grundrisse*. Marx gives us a language and categories that are essential to thinking about the capitalist system as a whole and to understanding the logic driving its reproduction.

Feminists, for instance, have appropriated Marx's analysis of the reproduction of labor power and have extended it to include reproductive activities that are absent in Marx but, nevertheless, are crucial to both capital's extraction of surplus labor and the reproduction of the class struggle.

However, no less than anti-colonial, antiracist critiques of Marx, a feminist perspective also indicates the limits of Marx's political theory. It shows that it is based on an exclusionary concept of work and revolutionary subjects, that it ignores the strategic importance of domestic work in the process of capitalist accumulation, and that it flattens gender-based differences into a disembodied conception of labor.

In this context, this book has a dual aim. On the one hand, it is to demonstrate that these are not minor omissions in Marx's work. By prioritizing capitalist production and waged labor as the central terrains of the class struggle and neglecting some of the most important activities by which our life is reproduced, Marx has only given us a partial view of the capitalist system and has underestimated its resilience and its capacity to mobilize sectors of the proletariat as instruments of both sexist and racist policies. In particular, undertheorizing reproductive work has affected his ability to anticipate crucial developments in capitalist strategy, such as the formation of a new proletarian family based on women's unpaid domestic work, which, coupled with substantial wage increases, by the turn of the twentieth century had become the basis of a new, informal sexual contract and a new patriarchal order, which I have defined the *patriarchy of the wage*, and which pacified large sectors of the male workforce. Indeed, much class antagonism has been deflated by men's ability to recuperate on the home front—at the expense of women—the power they lost in the workplace.

On the other hand, the book seeks to identify aspects Marx's analysis that are incompatible with a feminist anti-capitalist theory and political strategy, which arguably stands for a commitment to eliminate inequalities and all forms of exploitation. In pursuance of this task, the book revisits a set of issues that have been at the center of feminist studies and critiques of Marx. First, the question of "work" as the instrument of capitalist accumulation and the terrain of the confrontation between workers and capital. What enabled Marx and his followers to think of work only, or primarily, as industrial work and wage labor? In "Revolution Begins at Home,"[1] I briefly touch upon a historical reconstruction of the process by which, in mid-nineteenth-century Europe, waged labor became the only institutionally recognized form of work. The main argument running through the book, however, is that for a definition of what constitutes work a feminist perspective is all-important, for it makes visible the extent to which capitalism relies on unpaid labor, how it has turned every aspect of women's bodies and lives into forces of production, and how large areas of work in capitalist society are irreducible to mechanization, a challenge to Marx's belief that industrialization would drastically reduce necessary labor and free our time for higher pursuits.

A second key issue in the book is the question of the divisions that capitalism has created within the world proletariat, beginning with sexual and racial discrimination. In his writing and in his interventions as secretary of the First International, Marx denounced both patriarchal relations and racism, but we do not find in his work a serious analysis of the labor hierarchies capitalism has built in the course of his history, especially on the basis of "race" and "gender" and their consequences for an understanding of both the paths of capitalist development and class solidarity. Here too a feminist perspective is essential. It demonstrates that, *like racism and ageism, sexism is a structural element of capitalist development, that it is a material force standing in the way of any genuine social transformation, and that it cannot be eliminated (contrary to what Marx and Engels believed) by women entering the factories and working side by side with men.*

Not least, the book argues that feminists must be critical of the emancipatory role that Marx and the Marxist tradition after him have attributed to science, industry, and technology, whose development Marx described as capitalism's "historic mission."[2] Even more crucial, feminists must question the emancipatory role that Marx assigned to capitalism itself, which he considered the most rational organization of work and production and the highest form of social cooperation.[3] Together with his blindness to reproductive work and his underestimation of labor hierarchies and colonial relations, his belief in the ulti-mately "progressive" role of capitalism is undoubtedly the most problematic aspect of Marx's work. In the hands of twentieth-century socialists, it has made capitalist development the goal of the revolutionary process, in keeping with Lenin's argument that:

> The idea of seeking salvation for the working class in anything save the further development of capitalism is reactionary. In countries like Russia the working class suffers not so much from capitalism as from the insuf-ficient development of capitalism. The working class is, therefore, most certainly interested in the broadest, freest, and most rapid development of capitalism.[4]

Like Lenin, the whole Marxist tradition has assumed the inevitability and necessity of capitalism as a higher form of social organization, in that it increases social wealth, reduces necessary labor time, and through large-scale industrialization creates the material basis for communism. In reality, rather than building the material conditions for communist society (as Marx assumed they would), capitalist industry and technology have been destroying the earth, while at the same time creating new needs that make it difficult today to think of "revolution," for building a just society characterized by the equal sharing of natural and social wealth may involve reducing access to tech-nological tools that are becoming indispensable to our lives.

As I consistently state throughout this work, taking a criti-cal stand toward aspects of Marx's political theory is not to reject his work or to fail to recognize its importance. We are also learning now that Marx himself was often uncertain about his theories—that is presumably why he did not publish volumes 2 and 3 of *Capital* during his lifetime and left several revisions of his texts.[5] We also know that in his later years he revised his conception of the road to revolution, agreeing, in exchanges with Russian populists, that the Russian proletariat did not have to go through a capitalist phase in order to build communism but could transition to a communist society on the basis of the peasant commune, provided, however, that there was a revolution in Europe. In his later years, reading Lewis Morgan's *Ancient Society*, Marx also learned to appreciate the cultures and achievements of populations that lived at the preindustrial stage, for example, the native populations of the Americas.[6] Moreover, in an 1872 preface to the *Communist Manifesto*, together with Engels, he wrote that, contrary to their original opinion in 1848, "*One thing especially was proved by the [1871 Paris] Commune, viz., that 'the working class cannot simply lay hold of the ready-made state machinery and wield it for its own purposes.'*"[7] Thus, it is possible that he might also have reconsidered whether the working class could lay hold of capitalist technology and turn it to positive goals and, in time, may have also understood the importance of feminism, which he often dismissed as a struggle for bourgeois rights.

As for ourselves, the challenge is to imagine what contribution a reconstructed Marxism could make to the articulation of a feminist theory and a feminist political program. I will dedicate a second volume of this work to that project. Here, I will instead reconsider the main reasons for the difficult marriage between Marxism and feminism to date.

The essays that I have gathered in this volume include materials written over a long period of time: two in the mid-1970s, the rest during the past two decades. Each, then, represents a moment in the development of a feminist discourse on Marx and, at the same time, is an attempt to answer the question posed by Shahrzad Mojab: How do we overcome the "first great divide in history," join "two main emancipatory projects, Marxism and feminism," and provide the "breakthrough" that the politics of our time demand?[8]

"Counterplanning from the Kitchen" and "Capital and the Left," coauthored with Nicole Cox, belong to my period as a militant in the campaign for wages for housework, when our main task was, on the one hand, to respond to the critique of the left that insisted on defining domestic work as a residual element of a precapitalist world, and, on the other hand, to respond to libertarian feminists who described it, in an idyllic way, as the last outpost for the construction of family relations free from the dominance of the market and the interference of the state. The polemical tone of the two essays reflects the intensity of the debate our theses provoked, a debate that soon led me to reconstruct the history of capitalist development, partly, in fact, to explain the origin of domestic work and the specific character of sexual discrimination in capitalist society.

"Gender and Reproduction in Marx's *Capital*" was written more recently, partly stimulated by the new feminist interest in Marx and partly to demonstrate Marx's avoidance of any reference to women's reproductive work and his reduction of gender difference to a difference in the cost of labor.

"Marx, Feminism, and the Construction of the Commons" was a critical response to the Marxist autonomist theorization of a new phase of capitalist development, designated as "cognitive capitalism," presumably realizing Marx's prediction that capitalism creates the conditions for its own transcendence. Whereas Antonio Negri and Michael Hardt have looked at the digitalization of work as an instrument of increased workers' autonomy from capital, in my article I stress that digital technology today destroys what remains of the natural world fueling the extractivist drive that is destroying ecosystems across the world.

Finally, the last two chapters of the book, on "The Construction of Domestic Work in Nineteenth-Century England and the Patriarchy of the Wage" and "Origins and Development of Sexual Work in the United States and Britain," demonstrate the need to broaden Marx's concepts of capital's planning and of class struggle. Both examine the beginning of a new capitalist investment in the reproduction of the workforce at the turn of the twentieth century and a new state interest in the regulation of family relations and sexuality to give rise to a more productive working class. Both are evidence that, contrary to Marx's assumption, the reproduction of labor power is not accomplished by the market alone, and the class struggle is not fought only in the factories but also in our bodies, and it is fought not only between labor and capital but also within the proletariat, to the extent that men, especially when waged, have accepted being the state's representative within the family and the broader community with respect to women.

Notes

1   First published as "Revolution Begins at Home: Rethinking Marx, Reproduction and the Class Struggle," in Marcello Musto ed., *Marx's Capital After 150 Years: Critiques and Alternatives to Capitalism* (New York: Routledge, 2019).

2   Karl Marx, *Capital*, vol. 3 (London: Penguin, 1981 [1815]), 368.

3   As Marx wrote: "It is one of the civilizing aspects of capital that it extorts this surplus labor in a manner and in conditions that are more advantageous to social relations and to the creation of element for a new and higher formation than was the case under the earlier forms of slavery, serfdom etc."; ibid., 958.

4   V.I. Lenin, "Two Tactics of Social Democracy in the Democratic Revolution" (1905), in *Selected Works*, vol. 1 (New York: International Publishers, 1971), 486.

5   "[T]he late Marx was increasingly plagued by scholarly doubts about the stringency of his conceptual approach and desisted from publishing *Capital* vols. 2 and 3, despite being pressured from all sides"; Marcel van der Linden and Karl Heinz Roth, eds., *Beyond Marx. Theorizing the Global Labour Relations of the Twenty-First Century* (Leiden, NL: Brill, 2014), 7.

6   See Franklin Rosemont, "Karl Marx and the Iroquois," in *Arsenal: Surrealist Subversion* (Chicago: Black Swan Press, 1989), 201–13.

7   See Karl Marx and Frederick Engels, *The Communist Manifesto* (Harmondsworth, UK: Penguin Books, 1967), 54.

8   Sharzhad Mojab, *Marxism and Feminism* (London: Zed Books, 2015), 18.

ONE

Counterplanning from the Kitchen[1]

> Since Marx it has been clear that capital rules and develops through the wage. What has not been clear nor assumed by the organizations of the working class is that the exploitation of unwaged workers has also been organized through the wage. This exploitation has been even more effective because it has been hidden by the lack of a wage. Where women are concerned, our work appears to be a personal service outside of capital.
> —Mariarosa Dalla Costa and Selma James, 1975[2]

It is not an accident that over the last few months several left-wing journals have published attacks on Wages for Housework. The left realizes that this perspective has implications that go beyond the "woman question" and represents a break with its politics, past and present, both with respect to women and with respect to the rest of the working class. Indeed, the sectarianism the left has traditionally shown in relation to women's struggles is a consequence of its narrow understanding of the way capitalism rules and the direction our struggle must take to break this rule.

In the name of "class struggle" and "the unified interest of the class," the left has selected certain sectors of the working class as the revolutionary subjects and condemned others to a mere support role in the struggles these sectors were waging. *Thus, the left has reproduced in its organizational and strategic objectives the same divisions of the working class that characterize the capitalist division of labor.* In this instance, despite the variety of tactical positions, the left is united. When it comes to choosing the revolutionary subjects, Stalinists, Trotskyists, anarcholibertarians, the old and the new left, all join hands and form common cause around the same assumptions.

They Offer Us "Development"

Since the left has accepted the wage as the dividing line between work and nonwork, production and parasitism, the enormous amount of wageless work that women perform for capital in the home has escaped their analysis and strategy. From Lenin through Gramsci, the entire leftist tradition has agreed on the "marginality" of housework to the reproduction of capital and the marginality of the housewife to revolutionary struggle. According to the left, as housewives, women are not suffering from capitalist development but from the absence of it. Our problem, it seems, is that capital has not organized our kitchens and bedrooms, with the twofold consequence that we presumably work at a precapitalist stage and whatever we do in our kitchens and bedrooms is irrelevant to social change. Logically, if housework is outside of capital, our struggle against it will never cause capital to fall.

Why capital would allow so much unproductive work to survive is not a question the left has asked, confident of capital's irrationality and inability to plan. Thus, the outcome of an analysis that sees women's oppression as caused by exclusion from capitalist relations is a strategy advocating that we enter these relations, rather than destroy them. In this sense, there is an immediate connection between the strategy of the left for women and its strategy for the "Third World." In the same way as it wants to bring women into the factories, it wants to bring factories to the "Third World." In both cases, it presumes that the "underdeveloped"—i.e., those of us who are wageless and work at a lower level of technological development are backward with respect to the "real working class," and we can only catch up by gaining access to a more advanced form of capitalist exploitation, a bigger share of factory work. In both cases, the struggle the left offers to the wageless—the "underdeveloped"—is not a struggle against capital but a struggle for more rationalized, more productive forms of capitalist work. In our case, it offers us not only the "right to work" (this it offers to every worker) but the right to work more, that is, the right to be more exploited.

A New Ground of Struggle

The political foundation of Wages for Housework is precisely the refusal of this capitalist ideology, which equates wagelessness and low technological development with political backwardness, lack of power, and assumes that a precondition for our getting organized is that we are first organized by capital. It is our refusal to accept that because we are wageless or work at a lower technological level (these conditions are closely connected) our needs must be different from those of the rest of the working class. We refuse to accept that, while a male autoworker can struggle against the assembly line, starting from our kitchens in the metropolis or from the kitchens and fields of the "Third World," our goal must be the factory work that workers all over the world are now refusing. Our rejection of leftist ideology is one and the same as our rejection of capitalist development as a road to liberation or, more specifically, our rejection of capitalist relations whatever form they take. Inherent to this rejection is a redefinition of what capital is and who constitutes the working class, which is to say, a new evaluation of class forces and class needs.

Wages for housework, then, is not one demand among others; it is a political perspective that opens a new ground of struggle, beginning with women but for the entire working class.[3] This must be emphasized, since the reduction of wages for housework to a demand is a common element in the left's attacks on it, a way of discrediting it that avoids confronting the political issues it raises. In this sense, Carol Lopate's article, "Women and Pay for Housework" is one more example of reduction, distortion, and avoidance. The very title "Pay for Housework" misrepresents the issue. It ignores that a wage is not just a bit of money but the primary expression of the power relation between capital and the working class. It is in character that Lopate should invent a new formula to label a position that could never be stated in these terms. But perhaps this is due to the necessity she feels to be "hazy in our visions,"[4] which she firmly espouses as our female lot.

A subtler way of discrediting Wages for Housework is claiming that this perspective is imported from Italy and not relevant to the situation in the US, where women "do work."[5] Here is another example of misinformation. The "Power of Women and the Subversion of the Community"—the only source cited by Lopate—shows the international context in which this perspective originated. Moreover, tracing the geographical origins of Wages for Housework is irrelevant at the present stage of capital's international integration. What matters is its political genesis. *This is the refusal to see work and exploitation only in the presence of a wage.* It is the refusal of the distinction between women "who work" and women who are "just housewives," which implies that housework is not work, and that only in the US do women work and struggle, because so many of them have a second job. However, not to recognize women's work in the home because it is unwaged is to ignore that American capital was built on both slave labor and waged labor and, up to this day, thrives on the unwaged work of millions of women and men and children in the fields, kitchens, and prisons of the US and around the world.

The Hidden Work

Beginning with ourselves as women we realize that working for capital does not necessarily produce a paycheck and does not begin and end at the factory gates. As soon as we raise our heads from the socks we mend and the meals we cook and look at the totality of our workday, we see that while it does not receive a wage, our work produces the most precious product on the capitalist market: labor power. Housework, in fact, is much more than housecleaning. It is servicing the wage-workers physically, emotionally, and sexually and getting them ready to work day after day for the wage. It is taking care of our children—the future workers—assisting them from birth through their school years and ensuring that they too perform in the ways expected of them in capitalism. This means that behind every factory, every school, every office, and every mine there is the hidden work of millions of women, who consume their life reproducing those who work in those factories, schools, offices, and mines.[6]

The availability of a stable and well-disciplined labor force is an essential condition of production at every stage of capitalist development. This is why, to this day, in both "developed" and "underdeveloped" countries, housework and the family are the pillars of capitalist production. The conditions of our work vary from country to country. In some countries, we are forced into an intensive production of children; in others, we are told not to reproduce, particularly if we are black or on welfare or we reproduce "troublemakers." In some countries, we produce unskilled labor for the fields, in others, we produce skilled workers and technicians, but in every country the function we perform for capital is the same. Getting a waged job has never released us from housework. Having two jobs has only meant having less time and energy to struggle. Moreover, whether working full-time in the home or outside of it, whether married or single, we have to put hours of work into reproducing our own labor power, and we know the special tyranny of this task, since a pretty dress and a nice hairdo are conditions for getting the job, whether on the marriage market or on the wage labor market. Thus, we doubt that in the US

> schools, nurseries, daycare and television have taken away from mothers much of the responsibility for the socialization of their children[, and t]he decrease in house size and the mechanization of housework has meant that the housewife is potentially left with much greater leisure time.[7]

Among other things, day care and nurseries have never liberated any time for us but only time for additional work. As for technology, it is precisely in the US that we can measure the gap between the technology socially available and the technology that trickles into our kitchens. It is our wageless condition that determines the quantity and quality of the technology that we get. "If you are not paid by the hour, within certain limits, nobody cares how long it takes you to do your work."[8] If anything, the situation in the US proves that neither technology nor a second job can liberate women from housework and that:

> Producing a technician is not a less burdensome alternative to producing an unskilled worker if between these two tasks does not stand the refusal of women to work for free, whatever might be the technological level at which this work is done, the refusal of women to live in order to produce, whatever might be the particular type of child to be produced.[9]

Saying that the work we perform in the home is capitalist production is not the expression of a wish to be legitimated as part of the "productive forces." Only from the capitalist viewpoint can being productive be considered a moral virtue, not to say a moral imperative. From the point of view of the working class, being productive only means being exploited. "To be a productive laborer is, therefore, not a piece of luck but a misfortune."[10] Thus, we derive little "self-esteem" from it.[11] But when we say that housework—still our primary identification as women—is a moment of capitalist production, we clarify our function in the capitalist division of labor and the specific forms that our struggle against it must take. Our power does not come from anyone's recognition of our place in the cycle of production. Not production, but the power to withhold it, has always been the decisive factor in the social distribution of wealth. When we say that we produce capital, we say that we want to destroy it rather than fighting a losing battle to move from one form of exploitation to another.

We must also clarify that we are not "borrowing categories from the Marxist world."[12] Marx may never have dealt directly with housework. Yet we are less eager than Lopate to free ourselves from Marx, since Marx has given us an analysis that is irreplaceable for understanding how we function in capitalist society. We also suspect that Marx's apparent indifference to housework might be grounded in historical factors. By this we do not refer only to the dose of male chauvinism that Marx shared with his contemporaries (and not only with them). At the time when Marx was writing, the proletarian family centered on domestic work had yet to be created. What Marx had before his eyes were proletarian communities in which women were fully employed, along with their husband and children, each member of the family spending fifteen hours a day in a factory or other places of industrial work, and there was no time or space for "family life." It was only after terrible epidemics and overwork decimated the working class and, most importantly, after waves of proletarian struggles through the 1830s and 1840s brought England close to revolution, that the need for a more stable and disciplined workforce led capital to reconstruct the working-class family. Far from being a precapitalist structure, the family, as we know it in the West, is a creation of capital for capital, as an institution that is supposed to guarantee the quantity and quality of labor power and its control. "Like the trade union the family protects the worker but also ensures that he and she will never be anything but workers. And that is why the struggle of the woman of the working class against the family is crucial."[13]

Our Wagelessness as a Discipline

The family is essentially the institutionalization of our wageless labor, of our wageless dependence on men and, consequently, the institutionalization of a division within the working class that has disciplined men as well. For our wagelessness, our economic dependence, has kept men tied to their jobs, ensuring that whenever they wanted to refuse their work they would be faced with the wife and children who depended on their wages. Here is the basis of those "old habits—the men's and ours" that Lopate has found so difficult to break. It is no accident that it is difficult for a man "to ask for special time schedules so [that] he can be involved equally in childcare."[14] One reason that men cannot arrange for part-time hours is that the male wage is crucial for the survival of the family, even when the woman brings in a second wage. And if we "found ourselves preferring, or finding, less consuming jobs, which have left us more time for house-care," it is because we have resisted an intensified exploitation,[15] that of being consumed in a factory and then being consumed more rapidly at home. We also know that our wagelessness in the home is the primary cause of our weak position on the wage labor market. It is no accident that we get the lowest paid jobs, and that whenever women enter a male sector wages go down. Employers know that we are used to working for nothing and are so desperate for some money of our own that they can get us at a low price. Furthermore, the fact that housework is unwaged has given this socially imposed labor a natural appearance ("femininity") that affects us wherever we go and whatever we do. As housework and femininity have merged, as "female" has become synonymous with "housewife," we carry that identity and the "homely skills" we have acquired from birth to whatever job we take. This means that the road to the wage often leads us to more housework. Thus, we do not need to be told that "the essential thing to remember is that we are a SEX."[16] For years, capital has told us we are only good for sex and making babies. This is the sexual division of labor, and we refuse to make it eternal, which is inevitably what we are told when we ask: "What does being female actually mean? What, if any, specific qualities necessarily and for all time adhere to that characteristic?"[17] To ask these questions is to beg for a sexist and racist reply. Who is to say who we are? All we can find out now is who we are not, to the degree that we gain the power to break our imposed identity. It is the ruling class, or those who aspire to rule, who presuppose a natural and eternal human personality; this is to make their power over us eternal.

The Glorification of the Family

Not surprisingly, Lopate's quest for the essence of femaleness leads her to a blatant glorification of our unpaid labor in the home.

The home and the family have traditionally provided the only interstice of capitalist life in which people can possibly serve each other's needs out of love or care, even if it is often also out of fear and domination. Parents take care of children at least partly out of love. . . . I even think that this memory lingers on with us as we grow up so that we always retain with us as a kind of Utopia the work and caring which come out of love, rather than being based on financial reward.[18]

The literature of the women's movement has shown the devastating effects that this love, care, and service have had on women. These are the chains that have tied us to a condition of near slavery. We refuse to elevate to a utopia the misery of our mothers and grandmothers and our own misery as children! When the state does not pay a wage, it is those who are loved and cared for who must pay with their lives. We also refuse Lopate's suggestion that asking for financial reward "would only serve to obscure from us still further the possibilities of free and unalienated labor,"[19] which suggests that the quickest way to "dis-alienate" work is to do it for free. No doubt the capitalist class appreciates this suggestion. The voluntary labor on which the modern state rests is based on just such charitable dispensation of our time. It seems to us, however, that if instead of relying on love and care our mothers had received a financial reward, they would have been less bitter, less dependent, less blackmailed, and less inclined to blackmail their children, who were constantly reminded of their mothers' sacrifices. Our mothers would have had more time and power to struggle against their work and would have left us at a more advanced stage in that struggle.

It is the essence of capitalist ideology to glorify the family as a "private world," the last frontier where men and women can "keep [their] souls alive,"[20] and it is no wonder that this ideology is enjoying a renewed popularity with capitalist planners in our present times of "crisis," "austerity," and "hardship." As Russell Baker recently stated it in the *New York Times*, "love kept us warm during the Depression and we had better bring it with us on our present excursion into hard times."[21] This ideology, which opposes the family (or the community) to the factory, the personal to the social, the private to the public, productive to unproductive work, is functional to our enslavement to the home, which, to the extent that it is wageless, has always appeared as an act of love. This ideology has deep roots in the capitalist division of labor, which finds one of its clearest expressions in the organization of the nuclear family.

The way the wage relation has mystified the social function of the family is an extension of the way capital mystifies waged labor and the subordination of all social relations to the "cash nexus."

Marx clarified a long time ago that the wage hides all the unpaid work that goes into profit. But measuring work by the wage also hides the extent to which all our social relations have been subordinated to the relations of production, the extent to which every moment of our lives functions for the production and reproduction of capital. *The wage (including the lack of it), has allowed capital to obscure the real length of our workday.* Work appears as one compartment of life that takes place only in certain areas. The time we consume in the social factory, preparing ourselves for work or going to work, restoring our "muscles, nerves, bones and brains" with quick snacks, quick sex, movies, etc., all this appears as leisure, free time, individual choice.[22]

Different Labor Markets

Capital's use of the wage also obscures who the working class are and serves capital's need to divide in order to rule. Through the wage relation, not only has capital organized different labor markets (labor markets for blacks, for youth, for women, and for white males), but it has opposed a "working class" to a "non-working" proletariat, supposedly parasitic on the work of the former. As welfare recipients we are told that we live off the taxes of the "working class"; as housewives we are constantly pictured as bottomless pits for our husbands' paychecks. But, ultimately, the social weakness of the wageless is the weakness of the entire working class with respect to capital. As the history of the runaway shop demonstrates, a reserve of wageless labor both in the "underdeveloped" countries and in the metropoles has allowed capital to move away from those areas where labor had made itself too expensive, undermining the power that workers in these areas had achieved. Whenever capital could not run to the "Third World," it opened the gates of the factories to women, blacks, and youth or to migrants from the "Third World." It is no accident, in fact, that while capital is based on waged labor more than half of the world's population is still unwaged. Wagelessness and underdevelopment are essential elements of capitalist planning, nationally and internationally. They are powerful means to make workers compete on the national and international labor market and make us believe that our interests are different and contradictory. Here are the bases for the ideology of sexism, racism, and welfarism (to despise those workers who have succeeded in getting some money from the state) that are the direct expressions of different labor markets and, therefore, different ways of regulating and dividing the working class.[23] If we ignore this use of capitalist ideology and its roots in the wage relation, we not only end up by considering racism, sexism, and welfarism as moral diseases, a product of "miseducation" and "false consciousness," but we are confined to a strategy of "education" that leaves us with nothing but "moral imperatives to bolster our side."[24]

Finally we agree with Lopate when she says that our strategy relieves us from reliance on men being "good" to attain liberation.[25] As the struggles of black people in the sixties showed, it was not by good words but by organization of their power that black communities made their needs "understood." In our case, trying to educate men always meant that our struggle was privatized and fought in the solitude of our kitchens and bedrooms. There we could not find the power to confront capital. Power educates. First, men will fear, then they will learn, because capital will fear. For we are not struggling for a more equal redistribution of the same work. We are struggling to put an end to that work, and the first step is to put a price on it.

Wage Demands

Our power as women begins with the social struggle for the wage, not to be let into the wage relation (though we are unwaged, we were never outside of it) but to be let out, for every sector of the working class to be let out. Here we have to clarify the nature of wage struggles. When the left maintains that wage demands are "economistic," "union demands," they ignore that the wage, as well as the lack of it, is the measure of our exploitation and the direct expression of the power relation between capital and the working class and within the working class. They also ignore the fact that the wage struggle takes many forms and is not confined to wage raises. Reduction of work time, more and better social services, as well as money— all these are wage gains that determine how much of our labor is taken from us and how much power we have over our lives. This is why the wage has been the traditional ground of struggle between workers and capital. As an expression of class relations, the wage has two sides: the side of capital, which uses it to control us, by ensuring that every raise we gain is matched by an increase in productivity; and the side of the working class that is increasingly fighting for more money, more power, and less work. As the present capitalist crisis demonstrates, fewer workers are willing to sacrifice their lives at the service of capitalist production. Workers listen less and less to the calls for increased productivity. But when the "fair exchange" between wages and productivity is upset, the wage struggle becomes a direct attack on capital's profit and its capacity to extract surplus labor from us. Thus, *the struggle for the wage is at the same time a struggle against the wage*, for the power it expresses and against the capitalist relation it embodies. In the case of the unwaged, the struggle for the wage is even more clearly an attack on capital.

As such, wages for housework means that capital will have to pay for the enormous amount of social services that women now provide. Most important, to demand wages for housework is to refuse to accept our work as biological destiny. Nothing, in fact, has been so powerful in institutionalizing this work as the fact that not a wage but "love" has always been our pay. For us, as for waged workers, the wage is not a productivity deal. In return for a wage we will not work more than before. We want a wage in order to reclaim our time and energy and not have to be confined by a second job because we need financial independence.

Our struggle for the wage opens for the waged and the unwaged alike the question of the real length of the workday. Up to now, the working class, male and female, has had its workday defined by capital—from punching in to punching out. That defined the time we belonged to capital and the time we belonged to ourselves. But we have never belonged to ourselves. We have always belonged to capital every moment of our lives. And it is time that we make capital pay for every moment of it.

Making Capital Pay

This is the class perspective that has expressed itself in the streets in the struggles of the sixties, both in the US and internationally. In the US, the struggles of blacks and welfare mothers—the Third World of the metropolis—were the revolt of the wageless against the use capital had made of them and their refusal of the only alternative capital offered: more work. Those struggles, which had their center of power in the community were not for development but were for the reappropriation of the social wealth that capital has accumulated from both the wageless and the waged. In this sense, they fundamentally challenged the capitalist organization of society that imposes work as the only condition of our being allowed to live. They also challenged the leftist dogma that only in the factories can the working class organize its power. You do not need to enter a factory to be part of a working-class organization.

When Carol Lopate says that "the ideological preconditions for working-class solidarity are networks and connections which arise from working together," and "[t]hese preconditions cannot arise out of isolated women working in separate homes,"[26] she ignores the powerful struggles that these "isolated" women waged in the sixties. Furthermore, it is an illusion to think that capital does not divide us when we are not working in the isolation of our homes. In opposition to these divisions, we have to organize according to our needs. In this sense, Wages for Housework is as much a refusal of the socialization of the factory as a refusal of capital's rationalization and socialization of the home. We do not believe, in fact, that the revolution can be reduced to a consumer's report and a time-motion study, as is Lopate's proposal:

> [W]e need to look seriously at the tasks which are "necessary" to keep a house going. . . . We need to investigate the time and labor-saving devices and decide which are useful and which merely cause a further degradation of housework.[27]

But it is not technology that degrades us, but the use capital makes of it. Moreover, "self-management" and "workers' control" have always existed in the home. We always had a choice to do the laundry on Monday or Saturday and the choice between buying a dishwasher or a vacuum cleaner, provided we could afford them. Thus, we do not ask capital to change the nature of our work; we struggle to refuse reproducing ourselves and others as workers, as labor power, as commodities. A condition for achieving this goal is that this work be recognized as work with a wage. Obviously, as long as wages exist, so will capital. Thus, we do not say that gaining a wage is the revolution. We say, however, that it is a revolutionary strategy, for it undermines the role we are assigned in the capitalist division of labor and changes the power relations within the working class in terms more favorable to us and the unity of the class. As for the financial aspects of wages for housework, they are "highly problematical" only if we adopt the point of view of capital and the Treasury Department,[28] which always plead poverty when they confront the working class. Since we are not the Treasury Department and have no aspiration to be the Treasury Department, we cannot conceive of planning systems of payment, wage differentials, and productivity deals. It is not for us to put limits on our power. It is not for us to measure our value. It is only for us to struggle to get what we want, for us all. Our aim is to be priceless, to price ourselves out of the market, for housework and factory work and office work to become "uneconomic."

Similarly, we reject the argument that other sectors of the working class will have to pay for our eventual gain. According to this logic we could say, in reverse, that waged workers are now being paid with the money capital does not give to us. But this is the way the state talks. In fact, to say that the demands for social welfare programs by blacks in the sixties had a "devastating effect on any long-range strategy . . . on white-black relations," since "workers knew that they, not the corporations, ended up paying for those programs" is plain racism.[29] If we assume that every struggle inevitably ends up in a redistribution of poverty, we assume the defeat of the working class. Indeed, Lopate's article is written under the sign of defeatism, which is nothing other than accepting capitalist institutions as inevitable. Thus, Lopate cannot imagine that should capital try to lower other workers' wages to give us a wage, those workers will be able to defend their own interests as well as ours. She also assumes that "obviously, men would receive the highest wage for their work in the home"—in short, we will never win.[30] She sees housewives only as poor victims, so she cannot imagine that we could organize collectively to shut our doors in the face of any supervisor trying to control our work.

Notes

1   "Counterplanning from the Kitchen" was originally written in response to an article published in the journal *Liberation* by Carol Lopate; see Carol Lopate, "Women and Pay for Housework," *Liberation* 18, no. 8 (May–June 1974): 8–11. After the editors of the magazine rejected our reply, this and the following essay were published as a pamphlet by Falling Wall Press in Bristol: see Silvia Federici and Nicole Cox, *Counterplanning from the Kitchen: Wages for Housework: A Perspective on Capital and the Left* (Bristol: Falling Wall Press, 1975). The article was republished in Silvia Federici, *Revolution at Point Zero: Housework, Reproduction, and Feminist Struggle*, rev. ed. (Oakland: PM Press, 2020).

2   Mariarosa Dalla Costa and Selma James, *The Power of Women and the Subversion of the Community* (Bristol: Falling Wall Press, 1975), 27–28. The article was republished in Mariarosa Dalla Costa, *Women and the*

Subversion of the Community: A Mariarosa Dalla Costa Reader, ed. Camille Barbagallo (Oakland: PM Press, 2019).

3   See Silvia Federici, *Wages against Housework* (Bristol: Falling Wall Press, 1975); republished in Silvia Federici, *Revolution at Point Zero. Housework, Reproduction, and Feminist Struggle*, rev. ed. (Oakland: PM Press, 2020).

4   "We may have to be hazy in our visions. After all, a total reordering of sex and sexual roles and relationships is not easy to describe"; Lopate, "Women and Pay for Housework," 11. No worker is ever paid for her or his work, only for a (decreasing) portion of it. That is the essential feature of waged labor and capitalist exploitation.

5   "The demand to pay for housework comes from Italy, where the overwhelming majority of women in all classes still remain at home. In the United States, over half of all women do work"; ibid., 9.

6   Mariarosa Dalla Costa writes: "The community is essentially the woman's place in the sense that women appear and directly expend their labor there. But the factory is just as much the place where women's labor is embodied though they do not appear there but have transferred their labor to the men who work there. In the same way, the school embodies the labor of women who do not appear there but who have transferred their labor to the students who return every morning fed, cared for, and with clothes ironed by their mothers"; Mariarosa Dalla Costa, "Community, Factory and School from the Woman's Viewpoint," *L'Offensiva, Quaderni di Lotta Femminista*, no. 1 (Torino: Musolini Editore, 1972), 67.

7   Lopate, "Women and Pay for Housework," 9.

8   Dalla Costa and James, *The Power of Women and the Subversion of the Community*, 28–29.

9   Dalla Costa, "Community, School and Factory from the Woman's Viewpoint," 69; "Quartiere, scuola e fabbrica dal punto di vista della donna" In *L' Offensiva, Quaderni di Lotta Femminista* no. 1, Musolini Editore, 1972, 23–33

10 Karl Marx, *Capital*, vol. 1 (London: Penguin, 1981 [1867]), part 5, chapter 16.

11 "[I]t may well be that women need to be wage-earners in order to achieve the self-reliance and self-esteem which are the first steps toward equality"; Lopate, "Women and Pay for Housework," 9.

12 Ibid., 11.

13 Mariarosa Dalla Costa, "Women and the Subversion of the Community," in Dalla Costa and James, *The Power of Women and the Subversion of the Community*, 41.

14 "Most of us women who have fought in our own lives for such a restructuring have fallen into periodic despair. First, there were the old habits—the men's and ours—to break. Second, there were the real problems of time. . . . Ask any man how difficult it is for him to arrange part-time hours, or for him to ask for special time schedules so that he can be involved equally in childcare!"; Lopate, "Women and Pay for Housework," 11.

15   Ibid.

16   "The essential thing to remember is that we are a SEX. That is really the only word as yet developed to describe our commonalities"; ibid.

17   Ibid.

18   Ibid., 10.

19   "The elimination of the one large area of capitalist life where all transactions do not have exchange value would only serve to obscure from us still further the possibilities of free and unalienated labour"; ibid.

20   "I believe it is in our private worlds that we keep our souls alive"; ibid.

21   See Russell Baker, "Love and Potatoes," *New York Times*, November 25, 1974, 39.

22   Marx, *Capital*, vol. 1, 572.

23   See Selma James, *Sex, Race and Class* (Bristol: Falling Wall Press, 1975 [1972]).

24   Lopate, "Women and Pay for Housework," 11.

25   Ibid.

26   Ibid.

27   Ibid.

28   Ibid.

29   Ibid., 10.

30   Ibid.

TWO

Capital and the Left[1]

With its traditional blindness to the dynamics of class move-ments, the left has interpreted the end of a phase of the women's movement as the end of the movement itself. Thus, slowly but surely, they are trying to regain the political terrain that they were forced to relinquish in the sixties.

In the sixties, when women were leaving leftist groups in droves, the left had to espouse the validity of feminist autonomy. Reluctantly, they had to concede that women too are part of the revolution. They even went so far as to beat their breasts on their newly discovered sexism. Now, in the midst of what they perceive as a feminist funeral, their voices are raised again, this time to judge our achievements and shortcomings. Their story strikes us with a familiar ring. In the words of one of these self-appointed feminists, "women also need a socialist movement . . . and no movement that is composed only of women can substi-tute for this."[2] This means that it was all very well while it lasted but, ultimately, we have to be led by them, and to do that they want to reestablish the correct political line.

The Same Old Story
This, of course, is nothing new. Once again, we are told that serious politics are not kitchen business, and that our struggle to liberate ourselves as women—our struggle to destroy our work in the home, our relations in the family, the prostituting of our sexuality—is definitely subordinate, or at best auxiliary, to the "real class struggle" in the factories. Not accidentally, most of today's left polemics against feminist autonomy are dedicated

to denying that wages for housework is a feminist and, therefore, working-class strategy.

One plausible reason for this criticism is that if women have money of their own men may someday find their kitchens and beds empty. But a deeper reason is that leftists are not interested in freeing us from housework but only want to make our work more efficient. From their perspective, the revolution is a reorganization of capitalist production that will rationalize our exploitation instead of abolishing it.

This is why when we speak of "refusal of work" they immediately worry about "who will clean the streets." And this is why they always choose their "revolutionary subjects" from among those sectors of the working class whose work is more rationalized. That is to say, from their perspective, workers are revolutionary not because they fight against the exploitation but because they are producers. How far workers are from this perspective can be seen from the amount of energy the left spends reproaching them for their lack of "class consciousness." The left is horrified by the fact that workers, waged and unwaged, want more money and more time for themselves, instead of being concerned with how to rationalize production.

In our case, one thing is clear. The left attacks our struggle, because as houseworkers we do not measure up to the "productive" role they have assigned to the working class. What this means is well expressed by Wally Seccombe in the *New Left Review*:

> Revolutionary transformation is only possible because the proletariat is directly engaged in socialized labour and therefore bears as a class the prerequisite of a socialist mode of production. While the labour of housewives remains privatized they are unable to prefigure the new order or spearhead the productive forces in breaking the old.[3]

Seccombe concedes that in times of capitalist crisis (when capitalism is already falling apart, presumably on its own) "mobilization of housewives" around appropriate initiatives (e.g., price-watching committees) can make a contribution to the revolutionary struggle. "In such circumstances," he writes, "it is not uncommon that objectively backward layers of the working class be thrown forward." But the fact remains that "housewives will not provide the decisive motive force of women's struggle."[4] Since, internationally, the majority of women work first and above all as houseworkers this amounts to writing women out of the revolutionary process.

The Chinese Model

It is not the first time that "revolutionaries" have sent us back to the kitchen after a struggle has ended, this time with the promise of "sharing the housework." If this process is less evident today, that is because, in harmony with capital's plans, the same hand that is pushing us back into the home is also trying to push us into the factories to "join them in the class struggle" or, more accurately, to get ourselves trained for our future role in production.[5] The long-term arrangement they have for us is what they call the "Chinese model": socialization and rationalization of housework and self-management and self-control in the factories. In other words, a bit more of the factory in the home (higher efficiency and productivity of housework) and a bit more of the family in the factories (more individual responsibility and identification with work). In both cases, the left is espousing cherished capitalist utopias.

Self-management and self-control express the capitalist attempt to not only exploit the working class but to have it participate in planning its own exploitation. It is no accident that capitalist planners use the world "alienation" almost as often as the left and offer the same palliatives: "job enrichment," "workers' control," "workers' participation," "participatory democracy." As for the socialization and rationalization of housework (canteens, dormitories, etc.), capital has often toyed with this possibility, for, in terms of money, such rationalization would be a saving.

This was the plan in Russia, where speeding up the reproduction of labor power to free women's arms for the factories was one of the top priorities after the revolution. As in the dreams of the left, the guidelines that inspired the socialist planners was a "society of producers" where everything would be functional for production. From this point of view, the "house-commune," with its collective kitchens, diners, and lavatories, seemed the perfect solution to save money, space, time, and "raise the quality and productivity of labour."[6] It was only because of the obstinate resistance of the workers that these projects were increasingly abandoned.[7] Anatole Kopp reports on a women's assembly in Novisibirsk to demand "even a whole 5 square meters, provided it is individual space." By 1930, the Bolshevik urban planners had to recognize that:

> Everybody is disillusioned with the so-called "house-commune" . . . the "commune-con" where a worker's room is only big enough to sleep in. . . . The "commune-con" which cuts down living space and comfort (see the lines at the sink, toilet, dressing rooms, diners. . .) is beginning to rouse the dissatisfaction of the working masses.[8]

Since the 1930s, the Russian state has upheld the nuclear family as the most effective organism for disciplining workers and ensuring the supply of labor power, and, in China, despite a certain degree of socialization, the state also supports the nuclear family. In any case, the Russian experiment has demonstrated that when the goal is production and work, the socialization of housework can only mean a further regimentation of our lives—as the example of schools, hospitals, and barracks continuously teaches us. And this socialization by no means does away with the family; it simply extends it, in the form of "political and cultural committees" that exist at the community and factory level, as in Russia and China.

Given the factory, capital needs the family, or, more specifically, the discipline of the former is predicated on the discipline of the latter and vice versa. Nobody is born into this world a worker. This is why, whether dressed up in star-spangled banners or in hammers and sickles, at the heart of capitalism we always find the glorification of family life.

In the West, capital has been rationalizing and socializing housework for many years. The state has been planning the size, living conditions, housing, education, policing, drugging, and indoctrination of the family on an ever-increasing scale. That it has not been more successful is the result of the revolt of the wageless in the family—women and children. It is their revolt that has prevented the family from being more productive and, at times, even made it counterproductive. The left has been crying about this capitalist failure to discipline the family for a long time. As comrade Gramsci noted as early as 1919:

> All these factors make any form of regulation of sex and any attempt to create a new sexual ethic suited to the new method of production and work extremely complicated and difficult. However, it is still necessary to attempt this regulation and attempt to create a new ethic. . . . The truth is that the new type of man demanded by the rationalization of production and work cannot be developed until the sexual instinct has been suitably regulated and until it too has been rationalized.[9]

Today the left is more cautious but no less determined to tie us to the kitchen, whether in its present form or in a more rationalized, productive one. They do not want to abolish housework, because they do not want to abolish factory work. In our case, they would like us to do both. Here, however, the left confronts the same dilemma that troubles capital: Where can women be more productive, on the assembly line or on the baby line? Capital needs us in the factories as cheap labor, to replace other workers who are too expensive, but they also need us at home to keep potential troublemakers off the streets. The seeming difference between the Trotskyist line—housework is barbarism, i.e., all women to the factories—and the libertarian line—housework is socialism, i.e., no work should be paid—is only a difference of tactics within an overall capitalist strategy. The libertarians maintain that housework escapes socioeconomic categorization: "women's domestic labour under capitalism is neither productive nor unproductive"—Lisa Vogel;[10] "We may have to decide that housework is neither production nor consumption"—Carol Lopate;[11] "Housewives are and are not part of the working class"—Eli Zaretsky.[12] They place housework outside of capital and claim it is "socially necessary labor," because they believe that in one form or another it will also be necessary under socialism. Thus Lisa Vogel claims that domestic labor is primarily useful labor and "has the power under the right conditions to suggest a future society in which all labor would be primarily useful."[13] This is echoed by Lopate's vision of the family as the last retreat, where "we keep our souls alive."[14] And it culminates with Zaretsky's assertion that "housewives are integral to the working class and the working class movement not because they produce surplus value but because they perform socially necessary labor."[15]

In this context, we are not surprised to hear from Zaretsky that the tension between [feminism and socialism] . . . will continue well into the period of socialism . . . [because] with the establishment of a socialist regime class conflict and social antagonisms do not disappear, but instead often emerge in a sharper and clearer form."[16] Quite so. If this type of revolution occurs, we will be the first to struggle against it.

When, day after day, the left proposes what capital proposes, it would be irresponsible not to speak against it. The charge that wages for housework would institutionalize women in the home has come from every left group. Meanwhile, they rejoice that we are being institutionalized in the factories. At the moment when the women's liberation movement gave power to women institutionalized in both the home and the factory, the left has rushed to channel our subversion into yet another indispensable capitalist institution: the trade unions. This has now become the left wave of the future.

With this pamphlet we want to distinguish ourselves from the left with a class line. The knife that draws the line is feminist, but what it separates are not men from women but the technocracy from the working class it aims to supervise. We have been shy about speaking so plainly before now, but the left has blackmailed us with the charge of being for the state if we are not for them, in the same way as the American state has blackmailed the rebellious with the charge of communism, and the Russian state has blackmailed the rebellious with the charge of Trotskyism.

Goodbye to all that.

Notes

1   For an earlier version of this article, see "Capital and Gender," in *Reading "Capital" Today*, ed. Ingo Schmidt and Carlo Fanelli (London: Pluto Press, 2017).

2   Eli Zaretsky, "Socialist Politics and the Family," *Socialist Revolution* 3, no. 19 (January–March, 1974): 83–98.

3   Wally Seccombe, "The Housewife and Her Labour under Capitalism," *New Left Review* no. 83 (January–February 1974): 23.

4   Ibid., 24.

5   "[I]f men can be factory fodder why not women? . . . If we want to take our place in the world, to affect its history, we have to leave the safe confines of our homes and go into the factories . . . and help to take them over!"; *Workers Fight* no. 79 (December 1974–January 1975)

6   Anatole Kopp, *Città e Rivoluzione* (Milano: Feltrinelli, 1972 [1967]), 147.

7   Ibid., 160.

8   Ibid., 267.

9   Antonio Gramsci, "Americanism and Fordism," in *Selections from the Prison Notebooks* (London: Lawrence & Wishart, 1971), 277–318.

10 Lise Vogel, "The Earthly Family," *Radical America* 7, nos. 4–5 (July–October 1973): 28.

11 Carol Lopate, "Women and Pay for Housework," *Liberation* 18, no. 9 (May–June 1974): 11.

12 Zaretsky, "Socialist Politics and the Family," 89.

13 Vogel, "The Earthly Family, 26.

14 Lopate, "Women and Pay for Housework," 10.

15 Zaretsky, "Socialist Politics and the Family," 89.

16 Ibid., 83–84.

THREE

Gender and Reproduction in Marx's *Capital*[1]

As interest in Marxism and feminism is reviving and Marx's views on "gender" are receiving newfound attention, some areas of agreement among feminists are emerging that shape my approach to the subject.[2] It is generally agreed that although from his earliest works Marx denounced gender inequalities and patriarchal control of women, especially in the bourgeois family,[3] he "did not have much to say on gender and the family."[4] Taking "gender" to refer to the power relations between women and men, and the system of rules through which they are constructed and enforced, evidence shows that "gender" so defined is not an object of analysis in Marx's critique of political economy. Even in his main works, *Capital* and the *Grundrisse*, his views on the subject must be deduced from scattered observations.

Nevertheless, there is no doubt that Marx's work has made a major contribution to the development of feminist theory. In part, I agree with Martha Giménez that more than any statement that Marx made on women what counts for feminists is his methodology.[5] Not only has his historical and materialist method helped us deconstruct gender hierarchies and identities, demonstrating that "human nature" is a product of social action,[6] but his analysis of capitalism has given us the tools to think through the specific forms of exploitation to which women have been subjected in the capitalist organization of work and the relation between "sex, race, and class."[7] But the use that some of us have made of Marx has often taken diverged from the one he outlined.

Writing about gender in Marx, then, means coming to terms with two different perspectives on this subject. On the one hand, there are Marx's comments interspersed in his early works and in *Capital*, vol. 1; on the other, there are the views of feminists who have taken Marx's theories on the capitalist exploitation of labor and applied them to an analysis of women's work and the organization of reproduction, seeking to root feminism in an anti-capitalist/class perspective. Accordingly, I have divided what follows into two parts. In part 1, I examine Marx's views on "gender" as they can be construed from his analysis of women's employment in industrial labor in *Capital*, vol. 1. Here, I also comment on his silences, especially about women's relation to domestic work. I argue that Marx left the question of domestic labor untheorized because he believed that with the development of industrial production women's industrial employment would expand, and he also failed to see the strategic importance of reproductive work in all its different dimensions (domestic work, sex work, procreation) for the reproduction of the workforce and as a terrain of working-class struggle.

This has meant that, despite his condemnation of patriarchal relations, Marx has left us an analysis of capital and class that is conducted from a masculine point of view—that of the "working man," the predominantly white waged industrial worker in whose name the First International was formed, whose interest he assumed to be the interest of every sector of the proletariat. This has also meant that on the strength of this analysis many Marxists have felt justified treating gender as a "cultural" matter dissociated from the material conditions of the capitalist organization of work and have viewed feminists with suspicion, often accusing them of sowing divisions within the working class. Consequently, like the anti-colonial movement, the feminist movement had to start its theorizing with a critique of Marx, the full implications of which we are still discovering.

In part 2, I revisit this critique as it was developed first by the theorists of the Wages for Housework movement of which I was part.[8] Here, I argue that because we read Marx's analysis of capitalism "politically,"[9] we could expand Marx's theory of social reproduction, making it the foundation of a feminist theory centered on the redefinition of domestic work as the activity that produces "labor power" and, as such, as an essential condition of capitalist production and accumulation of wealth.

Reading Marx from a perspective inspired by the refusal of housework and "domesticity" showed us the limits of Marx's theoretical framework. It demonstrated that while feminists cannot ignore his work as long as capitalism remains the dominant mode of production, there are aspects of his political theory that we cannot accept, especially with regard to his concept of work and his assumptions concerning who qualifies as a worker and as a revolutionary subject.

Marx and Gender on the Industrial Shop Floor

Marx's conception of "gender" stands out most clearly in *Capital*, vol. 1, where for the first time he examined women's work in the factories, mines, and agricultural "gangs" during the industrial revolution. This was the "woman question" of the time on both sides of the channel, as economists, politicians, and philanthropists charged that women's factory work destroyed the family, made women excessively independent, usurped men's prerogatives, and contributed to workers' protest.[10] In France, the condition of the female factory worker, *"l'ouvrière,"* was

> at the forefront of debates on morality, economic organization, and the situation of the working classes. It also linked the concerns of political economy with the general debate on women that raged in this period.[11]

In England, reforms were already underway to limit women's and children's factory work by the time Marx began writing *Capital*. Thus, Marx could count on copious literature on the subject, mainly consisting of the reports compiled by the factory inspectors whom the government employed to ensure that the limits imposed were observed.[12]

Entire pages from these reports are cited in *Capital*, vol. 1, especially in the chapters on the "Working Day" and "Machinery and Large-Scale Industry," serving to illustrate the structural tendencies of capitalist production—e.g., the tendency to extend the workday to limit workers' physical resistance, to devalue labor power, and to extract the maximum of labor from the minimum number of workers. From these reports we learn about the plight of needlewomen dying of overwork and the lack of air and food,[13] about young girls working fourteen hours a day without meals or crawling half-naked into the mines to bring the coal to the surface, about children dragged from their beds in the middle of the night, "compelled to work for bare subsistence,"[14] "slaughtered" by a vampire-like machine, consuming their lives as long as "there remains a single muscle, sinew or drop of blood to be exploited."[15]

Few political writers have described in such uncompromising terms the brutality of capitalist work, outside of slavery, as Marx has done, and he must be praised for it. Particularly impressive is his denunciation of the barbaric exploitation of child labor, which remains unmatched in Marxist literature. But despite its eloquence, his account is generally more descriptive than analytic, and it is remarkable for the absence of a discussion of the gender questions that it raises.

We are *not* told, for instance, how the employment of women and children in the factories reshaped women's relations with men, how it affected workers' struggles, or what debates it prompted among workers' organizations. We have, instead, comments to the effect that factory labor degraded women's "moral character," by encouraging "promiscuous" behavior and making women neglect their maternal duties. Absent as well is any account of female factory workers as actors capable of fighting on their own behalf.[16] For the most part, female "factory hands" appear as victims, although their contemporaries noted their independence, their boisterous behavior, and their capacity to defend their interests against the factory owners' attempts to reform their ways.[17]

"Gender" and the Reproduction of the Workforce

Gender issues have a marginal place in *Capital*. In a three-volume text of thousands of pages, only on about one hundred do we find references to the family, sexuality, and domestic work, and these are generally passing observations. References to gender are missing even where we would most expect them, as in the chapters on the social division of labor, wages, and the reproduction of the workforce. When acknowledging the existence of a sexual division of labor in the family, Marx only observes that this has a physiological basis, neglecting to specify (against naturalizing justifications of "femininity" and family relations) that physiology is always apprehended and acted upon through the filter of social and cultural mediations.[18]

In the chapters on wages, after discussing the wage form and its concealment of the extraction of surplus labor, his main concern is clarifying the difference between the "nominal wage" and the "real wage" and the question of piecework. We do not find any mention of how the wage form hides the reproductive work that women do in the home and its contribution to the reproduction of labor power.

Marx recognizes that labor power, i.e., our capacity to work, is not a given. Daily consumed in the work process, it must be continuously regenerated, and this (re)production is as essential to the valorization of capital as "the cleaning of machinery," for "[i]t is the production of the capitalist's most precious means of production: the worker itself."[19] However, he places this production solely within the circuit of commodity production, the only exception being the activities involved in workers' training. Marx imagines that the workers buy with their wages the necessities of life and, then, by consuming them, reproduce themselves. What he describes then is literally a (re)production of waged workers by means of the commodities produced by them. Thus, "the value of labor power is the value of the means of subsistence necessary for the maintenance of its owner," determined by the labor time necessary for the production of the commodities that the workers consume.[20]

At no point, in *Capital* does Marx recognize that the reproduction of labor power requires some domestic work—preparing food, washing and mending clothes, cleaning, raising children, making love. "Domestic work" for him is what today we would call "homework," waged labor performed in the home.[21] No labor other than that required to produce the "means of subsistence" that workers' wages can buy is considered by Marx necessary to the reproduction of the worker's labor power or as contributing to its value. Thus, when considering the needs that workers must satisfy and their necessities for life, he only lists "food, clothing, fuel, and housing,"[22] awkwardly omitting sex, whether obtained in a familial set-up or purchased. He also ignores the fact that some of the most important commodities for the reproduction of labor power in Europe, those that fueled the Industrial Revolution (coffee, sugar, tobacco, cotton) were produced by slave labor on the American plantations.

In only a few passages does Marx break his silence on women's domestic work, though mostly referring to it as "family labor." In a footnote, in the chapter on "Machine and Large-Scale Industry," after noting that "capital for the purpose of its self-valorization, has usurped the family labor necessary for consumption,"[23] he commented:

> Since certain family functions, such as nursing and suckling children, cannot be entirely suppressed, the mothers who have been confiscated by capital must try substitutes of some sort. Domestic work, such as sewing and mending, must be replaced by the purchase of ready-made articles. Hence the diminished expenditure of labor in the house is accompanied by an increased expenditure of money outside. The cost of production of the working class therefore increases and balances its greater income. In addition to this, economy and judgment in the consumption and preparation of the means of subsistence becomes impossible.[24]

However, of this domestic work "that cannot be entirely suppressed" and has to be replaced by purchased goods, further reducing the family income, nothing more is said. Even when discussing the generational reproduction of the workforce, Marx makes no mention of women's contribution to it, referring to it as the "natural increase of the population," and commenting that "the capitalist may safely leave this to the workers' drives for self-preservation and propagation,"[25] although he must have known that proletarian women dreaded any new maternity and contraceptive methods were widely discussed among workers.

Why, Then, This Silence in Marx?

In trying to account for Marx's blindness to such ubiquitous form of work as housework, which must have unfolded daily under his eyes in his own home, in earlier essays I have stressed its near absence in proletarian communities at the time of Marx's writing, given that the entire family was employed in the factories from sunup to sundown.[26] Among Marxists, this is now the most common explanation,[27] and Marx himself invites this conclusion. Quoting a doctor sent by the English government to assess the state of health of the industrial districts, he noted that the shutting down of the cotton mills, caused by the American Civil War, had at least one beneficial effect. Women now

> had sufficient leisure to give their infants the breast instead of poisoning them with Godfrey's Cordial (an opiate). They also had the time to learn to cook. Unfortunately, the acquisition of this art occurred at a time when they had nothing to cook. . . . This crisis was also utilized to teach sewing to the daughters of the workers in sewing schools.

"An American revolution and a universal crisis were needed," Marx concluded, "in order that working girls, who spin for the whole world, might learn to sew!"[28]

Marx was certainly right about the collapse of housework skills among female factory hands, which even the bourgeoisie lamented, but the drastic reduction of the time and resources necessary for the workers' reproduction, which he and Engels documented, was not a universal condition. Factory workers were only 20 percent to 30 percent of the female working population; even among them, many abandoned factory work once they had a child. Moreover, by the mid–nineteenth century, female operatives had won a free Saturday afternoon. "Usurped by capital" as it may have been, domestic work in the industrial districts continued: at night and on Sundays, performed by youngsters or elderly women that female factory workers hired to care for their children. In addition, as we have seen, the conflict between factory work and women's "reproductive duties" was a key issue in Marx's times, as the factory reports he quoted and the reforms they produced demonstrate. By the 1830s, housework and the family were at the center of a lively discussion among socialists, anarchists, and the rising feminist movement.[29]

Reproductive activities had been an important subject for early socialist writers like Charles Fourier, who elaborated an ingenious theory to demonstrate that even the most laborious and unpleasant tasks could be turned into a play if placed into the hands of children.[30] More important, housework was a debated issue among Owenite socialist women who, in the 1830s and 1840s, widely discussed collective childcare, holding meetings to which thousands of people would come, "including many women often carrying their children in their arms."[31]

Why, Then, Again, This Silence in Marx?

No doubt, part of the answer is that Marx was not immune to the patriarchal tendency to consider women's reproductive work as a natural, instinctive, quasi-biological activity. That in the first phase of capitalist development women's reproductive work was only "formally subsumed" to capitalist production,[32] i.e., it was not yet reshaped to fit the specific needs of the labor market, possibly contributing to its naturalization. Yet as powerful a theoretician as Marx was, he should have realized that though housework appeared as an age-old, natural activity and a personal service, in reality, no less than the production of commodities, it was a historically specific type of work, a product of a separation between production and reproduction that had never existed in societies not governed by the law of exchange value, and essential, in proletarian communities, to the production of labor power.[33]

Was Marx silent on domestic work because he "did not see [the] social forces capable of transforming domestic labor in a revolutionary direction?" This is a legitimate question if we "read Marx politically," as Harry Cleaver has argued we must,[34] taking into account the fact that his theorizing was always concerned with organizational implications and potential.[35] It is also possible that he was guarded on the question of housework because he feared that attention to this work might play into the hand of workers' unions and bourgeois reformers that glorified domestic labor to justify the exclusion of women from industrial work.[36] But a more plausible answer is that Marx's disinterest in domestic work had deeper roots, stemming from his conception of what work is, what is valuable about it, and what forms of work are relevant to capitalist development and "the class struggle."

On the Concept of Work in Marx

"Work" in Marx refers to qualitatively different activities and social relations. It ranges from the "free activities" that are performed outside of any external constraint as realization of a conscious, self-determined purpose, allowing for the free play of our mental and physical powers—the highest form of work in his view, the one identifying our species-being and a primary need of our life—to the various forms of labor that satisfy our material needs.

There is obviously an immense difference for Marx between the activities that are performed out of necessity but are not exploitative and those that are performed under the compulsion of an external command. Of the former, Marx writes that "as creator of use values" "[l]abour is a condition of human existence which is independent of all forms of society; it is an eternal natural necessity which mediates the metabolism between man and nature, and therefore human life itself."

The latter, instead, is, for Marx, alienated labor, self-estrangement rather than self-realization.[37] Nevertheless, he looked positively at waged industrial work, attributing to it a formative character, arguing it equipped the workers with the skills, knowledge, attitudes required for the management of economic and social life.[38] Industrial work, moreover, is valued by Marx as a highly productive and cooperative form of work that can, once under the control of the workers, reduce the time and energy we must devote to the satisfaction of our needs and, thereby, liberate us for "higher activities,"[39] consisting, in Marx's description, of literary, artistic, and scientific pursuits—a far cry from the daily tasks of domestic work.

I propose that Marx ignored domestic work because it is neither a "free activity," in the sense that I have described, being thoroughly tainted by the necessity of survival, nor one capable of liberating us from toil, appearing instead as an archaic form of work, a vestigial heritage of societies, soon to be superseded by the progress of industrialization.

Marx never speculated about how reproductive work, and specifically housework, would be (re)organized under communism. Like Engels, he looked forward to a postcapitalist world in which, women would gain equality with men by joining them in the factories, and he praised industrialization for making it possible for women to enter "social production,"[40] in which presumably they had never participated.[41] In this spirit, at the end of the chapter on "Machinery and Large-Scale Industry," while discussing the introduction of elementary education for child factory workers, he wrote:

> However terrible and disgusting the dissolution of the old family within the capitalist system may appear, large scale industry, by assigning an important part in socially organized processes of production, outside the sphere of the domestic economy, to women, young persons and children of both sexes, does nevertheless create a new economic foundation for a higher form of the family and of relations between the sexes.[42]

Marx was mistaken in making this prediction. Threatened by class warfare and the possible extinction of the workforce, in England first, and then in the United States, in the same years as he was finishing the first volume of *Capital*, the capitalist class initiated a broad social reform, leading to the drastic reduction of female industrial labor and a reconstruction of the working-class family that deepened gender inequalities.

Marx did not anticipate this change. Though aware of the immense waste of life the capitalist system produced, he did not realize that what was at stake in the introduction of "protective legislation," by which women and children were gradually expelled from the factories, was more than a reform of factory work. Reducing the hours of female labor was the path to a new class strategy that reassigned proletarian women to the home, to cater to the daily and generational reproduction of the workforce. Through this move, capital was able to not only dispel the threat of working-class insurgency, again rising in the 1870s, but to create a new type of worker: stronger, more disciplined, more resilient, more apt to make the goals of the system his own—indeed the type of worker that would look at the requirements of capitalist production "as self-evident natural laws."[43] This was the kind of worker that enabled end-of-the-century British and US capitalism to make a technological and social shift from light to heavy industry, from textile to steel, from surplus labor extraction based upon the extension of the workday to one based upon a reduction of the workday compensated by the intensification of exploitation.

As I argue later in this volume,[44] the creation of the working-class family and the full-time proletarian housewife were an essential part of the transition from absolute to relative surplus. In this process, housework itself underwent a process of "real subsumption," for the first time becoming the object of a specific state initiative binding it more tightly to the need of the labor market and the capitalist discipline of work. Coinciding with the heyday of British imperial expansion (which brought immense riches to the country and also boosted workers' paychecks), this innovation was not the only factor responsible for the pacification of the workforce. But it was an epochal event, inaugurating the strategy that later culminated with Fordism and the New Deal, whereby the capitalist class would invest in the reproduction of labor power in order to create a more disciplined and productive workforce. This is the "deal" that lasted until the 1970s, when the rise of women's struggles internationally and the feminist movement put an end to it.

Feminism, Marxism, and the Question of Reproduction

While Marx, as proponent of "women's emancipation" through engagement in social production, generally understood as industrial labor, inspired generations of socialists, a different Marx was discovered in the 1970s by feminists who, in revolt against housework and economic dependence on men, turned to his work in search of a theory capable of explaining women's oppression from a class point of view. The result has been a theoretical revolution that has changed both Marxism and feminism.

Mariarosa Dalla Costa's analysis of domestic work as the key element in the production of labor power,[45] Selma James's location of the housewife on a continuum with a world of wageless proletarians who have nevertheless been central to capital accumulation,[46] their redefinition of the wage relation as an instrument for the naturalization and concealment of entire areas of exploitation: these theoretical developments and the discussions they generated have at times been described as the "housework debates," presumably centering on the question of whether or not housework is productive. This is a gross distortion. Discovering the centrality of women's unpaid labor in the home to the production of the workforce redefined not only domestic work but the nature of capitalism itself and the struggle against it.

It is not surprising that Marx's discussion of "simple reproduction" was a theoretical illumination in this process. Finding in Marx an argument that the activities that reproduce labor power are essential to capitalist accumulation brought out the class dimension of our refusal. It showed that this much-despised work, always taken for granted and dismissed by socialists as backward, has been in reality the pillar of the capitalist organization of work. This resolved the vexed question of the relationship between gender and class and gave us the tools to conceptualize not only the function of the family but also the depth of the class antagonism at the roots of capitalist society. From a practical point of view, it confirmed that, as women, we did not have to join men in the factories to be part of the working class and engage in an anti-capitalist struggle. We could struggle autonomously, starting from our own work in the home, as the "nerve center" of the production of the workforce.[47] And our struggle had to first be waged against the men of our own families, since through the male wage, marriage, and the ideology of love, capitalism has empowered men to supervise and command our unpaid labor and discipline our time and space. Ironically, then, our encounter with and appropriation of the Marxist analysis of the reproduction of labor power, while in a way consecrating Marx's importance for feminism also provided us with the conclusive evidence that we had to stand Marx on his head and begin our struggle precisely from that part of the "social factory" that he had excluded from his work.

Discovering the centrality of reproductive work for capital accumulation also raised the question of what a history of capitalist development would be like if seen not from the viewpoint of the formation of the waged proletariat but from the viewpoint of the kitchens and bedrooms in which labor power is daily and generationally produced. The need for a gendered perspective on the history of capitalism—beyond "women's history" or the history of waged labor—is what led me, among others, to rethink Marx's account of primitive accumulation and discover the sixteenth- and seventeenth-century witch-hunts as foundational moments in the devaluation of women's labor and the rise of a specifically capitalist sexual division of work.[48] The simultaneous realization that, contrary to Marx's anticipation, primitive accumulation had become a permanent process has also called into question Marx's conception of capitalist development as a necessary condition for the construction of a communist society. It has invalidated Marx's stadial view of history, in which capitalism is depicted as the purgatory that we must inhabit on the way to freedom.

The rise of eco-feminism, which has connected Marx's devaluation of women's labor and reproduction with his view that humanity's historic mission is the domination of nature, strengthened our stand. The work of Maria Mies and Ariel Salleh, which has demonstrated that Marx's effacement of reproductive activities is not an accidental element contingent to the tasks he assigned to them in *Capital* but a systemic one, has been especially important. As Salleh put it:

> [E]verything in Marx establishes that what is created by man and technology has a higher value: history begins with the first act of production, human beings realize themselves through work, a measure of their self-realization is their capacity to dominate nature and adapt it to human needs, and all positive transformative activities are thought in the masculine: labor is described as the father, nature as the mother.[49]

The earth too is seen as feminine—*Madame la Terre*, Marx calls it, against *Monsieur le Capital*.

Today the miscalculation that Marx and generations of Marxist socialists have made with regard to the liberating effects of industrialization are all too obvious. No one would dare to dream—as August Bebel did in *Woman under Socialism* (1903)—of the day when all food would be chemically produced and everyone would carry a little box of chemicals wherewith to provide their food supply of albumen, fat, and hydrates of carbon, regardless of the hour of the day or the season of the year.[50] As industrialization, now in its new digital form, is eating the earth, and scientists at the service of capitalist development are tinkering with the production of life outside of the bodies of women, the idea of extending industrialization to all our reproductive activities and every corner of the world is a nightmare worse than the one we are already experiencing with the full industrialization of agriculture.

Not surprisingly, we have been witnessing a "paradigm shift" in radical circles, as hope in the machine as a driving force of "historical progress" is being displaced by a refocusing of political work on the issues, values, and relations arising from the reproduction of our lives and the life of the ecosystems in which we live. We are told that in the last years of his life Marx too reconsidered his historical perspective and, on reading about the egalitarian, matrilineal communities of the American Northeast, he began to reconsider his idealization of capitalist industrial development and to appreciate the power of women.[51] Nevertheless, the Promethean view of technological development that Marx and the entire Marxist tradition have promoted, far from losing its attraction, is making a comeback, with digital technology playing for some the same emancipatory role that Marx assigned to automation, such that the world of reproduction and care work—which feminists have valorized as a terrain of transformation and struggle—risks being overshadowed once again. That is why, although Marx devoted limited space to the question of "gender" in his work and may have changed some of his views in later years, it is important to stress, as I have tried to do in this essay, that his silence on this matter is not an oversight but the sign of a limit that his theoretical and political work could not overcome but that ours must.

Notes

1   "Gender and Reproduction in Marx's *Capital*" was originally published as "Capital and Gender," in Ingo Schmidt and Carlo Fanelli, eds., *Reading 'Capital' Today* (London: Pluto Press, 2017).

2   Signs of the renewed interest in Marx's theory of gender include the publication of Heather A. Brown, *Marx on Gender and the Family* (London: Brill, 2012) and Shahrzad Mojab, ed., *Marxism and Feminism* (London: Pluto Press, 2015), the latter published in conjunction with the conference organized on the subject by the Rosa Luxembourg Foundation in Berlin that year; also see Martha E. Giménez, *Marx, Women and Capitalist Social Reproduction* (Chicago: Haymarket, 2018).

3   In the *Economic and Philosophical Manuscripts of 1844*, echoing Charles Fourier, Marx argued that the man-woman relation is a measure of social progress; it tells us the extent to which man has humanized his nature. In the *German Ideology*, he spoke of the "slavery latent in the family," based upon the father's appropriation of the labor of women and children. In his translation of Jaques Peuchet's essay "On Suicide," he showed the destructive consequences of bourgeois morality on women's lives. Again, in the *Communist Manifesto*, he derided the bourgeois family, arguing that it was built on adultery, within which women only served the transmission of private property.

4   Brown, *Marx on Gender and the Family*, 143; also see Frigga Haug, "The Marx within Feminism," in Mojab, *Marxism and Feminism*, 76–101. As Haug writes, "Marx's analysis [is] remarkable for a certain vacuity and silence on the subject of women"; ibid., 81.

5   Giménez, *Marx, Women and Capitalist Social Reproduction*, 247.

6   Nancy Holmstrom, "A Marxist Theory of Women's Nature," *Ethics* 94, no. 3 (1984): 456–73.

7   The quotes here refer to Selma James, *Sex, Race and Class* (Bristol: Falling Wall Press, 1975).

8   Classic works from the Wages for Housework movement include: Mariarosa Dalla Costa, "Women and the Subversion of the Community," in Mariarosa Dalla Costa and Selma James, *The Power of Women and the Subversion of the Community* (Bristol: Falling Wall Press, 1975); Selma James, *Sex, Race and Class*; Leopoldina Fortunati, *The Arcane of Reproduction: Housework, Prostitution, Labor and Capital* (Brooklyn: Autonomedia, 1995 [1981]). For a history of the New York branch of the movement see Silvia Federici and Arlen Austin, eds., *The New York Wages for Housework Committee: History, Theory, Documents, 1972–1977* (Brooklyn: Autonomedia, 2019).

9   The reference here is to Harry Cleaver, *Reading Capital Politically* (Leeds: Anti/Thesis, 2000 [1979]).

10   On the debate about the consequences of women's industrial labor as the "woman question" in nineteenth-century England, see Judy Lown, *Women and Industrialization: Gender at Work in Nineteenth-Century England* (Minneapolis: University of Minnesota Press, 1990), 1–4, 131, 213–18. For the same debates in France, see Joan Wallach Scott, *Gender and the Politics of History* (New York: Columbia University Press, 1988), 139–66.

11   Scott, *Gender and the Politics of History*, 140.

12   On the reform of female and child labor in England, besides Marx, *Capital* vol. 1 (London: Penguin, 1981 [1867]), see Lown, *Women and Industrialization*, 180–84.

13   Marx, *Capital*, vol. 1, 365.

14   Ibid., 353.

15   Ibid., 416.

16   The only reference to a female factory workers' struggle is in a note in *Capital* vol. 1, where Marx mentions power loom weavers going on strike in Wiltshire over the question of timekeeping; ibid., 551.

17   For an account of female factory worker struggles in nineteenth-century England, see Margaret Hewitt, *Wives and Mothers in Victorian Industry: A Study of the Effects of the Employment of Married Women in Victorian Industry* (London: Rockliff, 1958); Judy Lown, who speaks of female workers' opposition to proposed Factory Acts in the 1830s (Lown, *Women and Industrialization*, 214) and of silk workers' struggle "to maintain control over those aspects of life which had always been central to working women's experience . . . childcare, personal hygiene and dress" (ibid., 162). On factory girls "representing a newly found independence and freedom for womankind," see ibid., 43ff.; Wally Seccombe, "The Housewife and Her Labour under Capitalism," *New Left Review*, no. 83 (January–February 1974): 121.

18   As Marx writes: "Within a family . . . there springs up naturally a division of labour caused by differences of sex and age, and therefore based upon a pure physiological foundation"; Marx, *Capital*, vol. 1, 471.

19   Ibid., 718. Marx returns to this question in Karl Marx, *Theories of Surplus Value, Part 1* (Moscow: Progress Publishers, 1969 [1862–1863]), 172, where

he argues: "Productive labour would therefore be such labour that produces commodities or directly produces, trains, develops, maintains, or
reproduces labour power itself."

20   Marx, *Capital*, vol. 1, 274, 276, 340.

21   As Frigga Haug has pointed out, "Marx and Engels conceptualized
housework primarily as wage labor, performed in the home, treating as
'family work' what in the twentieth century has generally been understood as housework"; Haug, "The Marx within Feminism," 91.

22   Marx, *Capital*, vol. 1, 275.

23   Ibid., 518n38.

24   Ibid., 518n39.

25   Ibid., 718.

26   Silvia Federici, "The Reproduction of Labor Power in the Global
Economy," in *Revolution at Point Zero: Housework, Reproduction, and
Feminist* Struggle, rev. ed. (Oakland: PM Press, 2020), 104.

27   See, for instance, John Bellamy Foster, "Women, Nature and Capital in
the Industrial Revolution," *Monthly Review* 69, no. 8 (January 2018): 2.

28   Marx, *Capital*, vol. 1, 517–18n38

29   On this topic, see Wallach Scott, *Gender and the Politics of History*, 94–95;
Dolores Hayden, *The Grand Domestic Revolution* (Cambridge: MIT Press,
1982), 1–8. Wallach Scott writes that "the literature of protest of the
1830s and 1840s is full of references to the family and to the traits of
men and women. Whether one reads about demands for higher wages
or attacks on the cupidity of the bourgeoisie, whether one listens as
speakers evoke the depth of worker poverty or as they raise their glasses
to toast a future new society, one hears about sexual difference. In the
program of utopian socialists of the period, the family was a central
theme whether, as with Charles Fourier and the Saint-Simonians, experiments with altered forms of family organization were posed, or as with
Etienne Cabet, promises of qualitative improvement in the happiness
of traditional couples and their children. The organization of labor and
association were only two of the themes in this period of working class
protest; the family was an equally important and interrelated third";
Scott, *Gender and the Politics of History*, 94–95.

30   Charles Fourier, *Design for Utopia: Selected Writings of Charles Fourier*
(New York: Shocken Books, 1971), 171–76.

31   Barbara Taylor, "The Men Are as Bad as Their Masters . . .": Socialism,
Feminism, and Sexual Antagonism in the London Tailoring Trade in the
Early 1830s," *Feminist Studies* 5, no. 1 (1979): 10–12.

32   Marx's uses the concept of "formal," versus "real," subsumption to
describe the process whereby, in the first phase of capitalist accumulation, capital appropriates labor "as it finds it," "without any modification
in the real nature of the labor process"; *Capital*, vol. 1, 1021. By contrast,
we have "real subsumption" when capital shapes the labor/production
process directly for its own ends. It was with the introduction of the
"family wage," and the reconstruction of the proletarian family in the
decades between the 1870s and World War 1 that such transformation

occurred. However, as Harry Cleaver pointed out in a letter commenting on this article, we should not overestimate the change. As he pointed out, "Like in the work of producing commodities other than labor-power, history shows a decided mixed evolution with lots of coexistence among modes. For example, while it would be a long time before the capitalists became actively engaged in teaching 'home economics,' they were quite actively involved in organizing workers' housing, as Engels described in *The Condition of the Working Class in England* (1845) and later in *The Housing Question* (1872)."

33   On this topic, see Fortunati, *The Arcane of Reproduction*; also see Silvia Federici, *Caliban and the Witch* (Brooklyn: Autonomedia, 2004), especially chapter 2.

34   My reference here is to Cleaver, *Reading Marx Politically*, 58.

35   This is a point on which Negri insists in Antonio Negri, *Marx beyond Marx: Lessons on the Grundrisse*, ed. Jim Fleming, trans. Harry Cleaver (Brooklyn: Autonomedia, 1991), 182.

36   As Wally Seccombe, among others, documents, even among trade unions the demand for higher workers' wages was often fought with the argument that their wives could return to their proper role; Wally Seccombe, *Weathering the Storm: Working-Class Families from the Industrial Revolution to the Fertility Decline* (London: Verso, 1993), 114–19.

37   On "alienated labor," see Karl Marx, *Economic and Philosophical Manuscripts of 1844*, trans. Martin Milligan (Moscow: Foreign Languages Publishing House, 1961).

38   Marx's view of industrial labor as a more rational, more educational (in the broad sense of the word) type of work recalls what Alfred Marshall, the father of marginal theory, in his *Principles of Economics* (1890), later called a "general ability to work," which he described as a new capacity, possessed, in his time, by few workers in the world and "not peculiar to any occupation" but wanted by all, "enabling workers to keep at any kind of work for a long time, bear in mind many things at a time . . . accommodate quickly to changes in detail of the work done, to be steady and trustworthy." Marshall, however, in line with nineteenth-century reformers, insisted that the prime contributor to the production of this "general ability" was "home-life and especially the mother," which was the reason why he opposed women's external employment. Marx, by contrast, is silent on the work of mothering, only observing its absence, and, more broadly, is silent on the potential of reproductive work as a basis for workers resistance; Alfred Marshall, *Principles of Economics: An Introductory Volume* (London: Macmillan and Co., 1938), 206–7.

39   On industrial work as promoting cooperation, raising the productivity of labor, thereby, shortening the time needed to produce commodities, and as an equalizer, see Marx, *Capital* vol. 1, 517, 526, 545.

40   Ibid., 739.

41   However Gisela Boch and Barbara Duden have argued that there is no historical basis for the idea, to which Marx and other socialists

subscribed, that the development of capitalism "with its increasingly industrial work of women, freed and frees them from the age-old feudal reigns of housework and tutelage by men"; Gisela Boch and Barbara Duden, "Labor of Love—Love as Labor: On the Genesis of Housework in Capitalism," in Edith Hoshino Altback, ed., *From Feminism to Liberation* (Cambridge: Schenkman Publishing, 1980), 157. It is also highly questionable that women were drawn into industrial labor by its reduction of the need for physical strength. The description that Marx himself gives us of women and children's employment in the mines, as in in the factory system, should dispose of that assumption.

42 Marx, *Capital*, vol. 1, 620–21.

43 Ibid., 899.

44 See the chapter "The Construction of Domestic Work in Nineteenth-Century England and the Patriarchy of the Wage," pages 96–107, in this volume.

45 Dalla Costa, "Women and the Subversion of the Community," 31.

46 James, *Sex, Race and Class*.

47 Fortunati, *The Arcane of Reproduction*, 125.

48 Federici, *Caliban and the Witch*, 92–102.

49 Ariel Salleh, *Ecofeminism as Politics: Nature, Marx and the Postmodern* (London: Zed Books, 1997), 72–76.

50 August Bebel, *Woman under Socialism* (New York: Schocken Books, 1971 [1183]), 287–88.

51 On this topic, see the discussion of Karl Marx's *Ethnological Notebooks* in Brown, *Marx on Gender and the Family*, chapters 6 and 7.

FOUR

Marx, Feminism, and the Construction of the Commons[1]

> Communism is for us not a state of affairs which is to be
> established, an ideal to which reality will have to adjust
> itself. We call communism the real movement which
> abolishes the present state of things, The conditions of
> this movement result from the premises now in existence.
> —Karl Marx and Frederick Engels, *The German Ideology*[2]

Introduction

What tools, principles, and ideas can Marxism bring to feminist
theory and politics in our time? Can we think today of a relation between Marxism and feminism other than the "unhappy
marriage" that Heidi Hartman depicted in a much-quoted
1979 essay?[3] What aspects of Marxism are most important for
reimagining feminism and communism in the twenty-first
century? How does Marx's concept of communism compare
with the principle of the commons, the political paradigm
inspiring so much radical feminist thinking today?

In asking these questions, I join a conversation on the construction of alternatives to capitalism that has begun in encamp-
ments and squares across the planet where, in ways replete with
contradictions but also with new creative possibilities, a society
of "commoners" is coming into existence, striving to build
social spaces and relations not governed by the logic of the
capitalist market.

Assessing the legacy of Marx's vision of communism for
the twenty-first century is not an easy task, however. Added
to the complexity of Marx's thought is the fact that in the last

period of his life, after the defeat of the Paris Commune, Marx apparently abandoned some of his political axioms, especially with regard to the material preconditions for the construction of a communist society.[4] It is also argued that there are important differences between his two major works, *Capital* and the *Grundrisse*,[5] and, above all, that Marx is not a writer whose thought can be grasped through any fixed set of formulations, as "his level of analysis [was] continuously changing with his political design."[6]

Two Things, However, Are Certain

The political language that Marx has given us is still necessary to think of a world beyond capitalism. His analysis of surplus value, money, and the commodity form, and, above all, his method— giving history and the class struggle a material foundation, and refusing to separate the economic from the political—are still indispensable, though not sufficient, for understanding contemporary capitalism. Not surprisingly, with the deepening of the global economic crisis there has been a revival of interest in Marx's work that many could not have anticipated in the 1990s, when the dominant wisdom declared his theory defunct. Instead, amid the debris of actually existing socialism, broad debates have emerged on the questions of "primitive accumulation," the modalities of the "transition," and the historical and ethical meaning and possibility of communism. Mixed with feminist, anarchist, antiracist, and queer principles, Marx's theory continues to influence the rebels of Europe, the Americas, and beyond. An anti-capitalist feminism cannot ignore Marx. Indeed, as Stevi Jackson has argued, "until the early 1980s the dominant perspectives within feminist theory were generally informed by, or formulated in dialogue with Marxism."[7] However, there is no doubt that Marx's categories must be given new foundations and we must go "beyond Marx."[8] This is not only because of the social and economic transformations that have taken place since Marx's time, but also because of the limits in his understanding of capitalist relations—limits whose political significance has been made visible by the social movements of the last half a century, which have brought to the world stage social subjects that Marx's theory ignored or marginalized.

Feminism and the Viewpoint of Social Reproduction

Feminists have made an important contribution to this process, but they have not been alone. In the 1950s and 1960s, in the wake of the anti-colonial struggle, political theorists like Frantz Fanon questioned an analysis that, like Marx's, has almost exclusively focused on wage labor and assumed the vanguard role of the metropolitan industrial proletariat,[9] thus marginalizing the place of the enslaved, the colonized, and the unwaged in the process of accumulation and anti-capitalist struggle. These political theorists realized that the experience of the colonies called for a rethinking "of Marxism as a whole," and either Marxist theory would have to be reframed to incorporate the experiences of the 75 percent of the world population, or it would cease to be a liberating force and become instead an obstacle to revolutionary change.[10] For the peasants, the peones, and the lumpen who made the revolutions of the twentieth century showed no intention of waiting for a future proletarianization or for "the development of the productive forces" to demand a new world order, as orthodox Marxists and the parties of the left advised them to do. In turn, black revolutionaries in the United States, from W.E.B. Du Bois to Cedric Robinson, have stressed the absence in Marx's work of an analysis of racial inequalities as a structural characteristic of capitalist society and the capitalist exploitation of labor.[11]

Ecologists, including some eco-socialists, have also taken Marx to task for promoting an asymmetrical and instrumental view of the man-nature relation, presenting human beings and labor as the only active agents and denying nature any intrinsic value and self-organizing potential.[12] But it was with the rise of the feminist movement that a more systematic critique of Marxism could be articulated, for feminists have brought to the table not only the wageless of the world but the vast population of social subjects (women, children, occasionally men) whose daily work in fields, kitchens, and bedrooms produces and reproduces the workforce and, with it, a set of issues and struggles on the terrain of social reproduction that Marx and the Marxist political tradition have barely touched upon.

It is starting from this critique that I consider the legacy of Marx's vision of communism, concentrating on those aspects that are most important for a feminist program and for the politics of the commons, by which I refer to the many practices and perspectives embraced by social movements across the planet that today seek to enhance social cooperation, undermine the market's and state's control of our lives, and put an end to capital accumulation. Anticipating my conclusions, I argue that Marx's vision of communism as a society beyond exchange value, private property, and money, based on associations of free producers and governed by the principle "from each according to their ability, to each according to their needs" represents an ideal that no anti-capitalist feminist can object to. Feminists can also embrace Marx's inspiring image of a world beyond the social division of labor, although we may want to ensure that between hunting in the morning, fishing in the afternoon, and criticizing after dinner—Marx's vision of the good life in a postcapitalist society—there will be time for everyone to share cleaning and childcare.

However, far more important for feminist politics than any ideal projection of a postcapitalist society are Marx's relentless critique of capitalist accumulation and his methodology, beginning with his reading of capitalist development as the product of antagonistic social relations. In other words, as Roman Rosdolsky and Antonio Negri,[13] among others, have argued, more than the visionary revolutionary projecting a world of achieved liberation, the Marx who most matters to us is the theorist of class struggle, who refused any political program not rooted in real historical possibilities and throughout his work pursued the destruction of capitalist relations, seeing the realization of communism in the movement that abolishes the present state of things. From this point of view, Marx's historical materialist method, which posits that in order to understand history and society we must understand the material conditions of social reproduction, is crucial for a feminist perspective. Recognizing that social subordination is a historical product, rooted in a specific organization of work has had a liberating effect on women. It has denaturalized the sexual division of labor and the identities built upon it, projecting gender categories not only as social constructs but also as concepts whose content is constantly redefined, infinitely mobile, open-ended, and always politically charged. Indeed, many feminist debates on the validity of "women" as an analytic and political category could be more easily resolved if this method were applied, for it teaches us that it is possible to express a common interest without ascribing fixed and uniform forms of behavior and social condition.

Analyzing the social position of women through the prism of the capitalist exploitation of labor also discloses the continuity between discrimination on the basis of gender and discrimination on the basis of race and enables us to transcend the politics of rights that assumes the permanence of the existing social order and fails to confront the antagonistic social forces standing in the way of women's liberation.

However, as many feminists have shown, Marx did not consistently apply his own method, at least not to the question of reproduction and gender relations. As both the theorists of the Wages for Housework movement—Mariarosa Dalla Costa, Selma James, Leopoldina Fortunati[14]—and eco-feminist theorists—Maria Mies and Ariel Salleh[15]—have demonstrated, there is a contradiction at the center of Marx's thought. Although he takes the exploitation of labor as the key element in the production of capitalist wealth, he leaves untheorized some of the activities and social relations that are most essential for the production of labor power, including sexual work, procreation, childcare, and domestic work. Marx acknowledged that our capacity to work is not a given but is a product of social activity that always takes a specific historical form,[16] for "hunger is hunger, but the hunger that is satisfied by cooked meat eaten with knife and fork is different from the hunger that devours raw meat with the help of hands, nails and teeth."[17] Nevertheless, we do not find in his published work any analysis of domestic labor, the family and the gender relations specific to capitalism, except for scattered reflections to the effect that the first division of labor was in the sexual act,[18] that slavery is latent in the family,[19] and so forth. Domestic work is dealt with in two footnotes, one registering its disappearance from the homes of the overworked female factory hands, and the other noting that the crisis caused by the American Civil War brought the female textile workers in England back to their domestic duties.[20] Procreation is also underplayed and generally treated as a natural function rather than a form of labor that in capitalism is subsumed to the reproduction of the workforce and, therefore, subject to a specific state regulation.[21]

Because of these omissions many feminists have viewed feminism's relation to Marxism as a process of subordination.[22] The authors I have quoted, however, have demonstrated that we can work with Marx's categories but must reconstruct them and change their architectural order, so that their center of gravity is not exclusively waged labor or commodity production but includes the production and reproduction of labor power and especially that part of it that is carried out by women within the home. In doing so, we make visible a key terrain of accumulation and struggle, as well as the full extent of capital's dependence on unpaid labor and the full length of the workday.[23] Indeed, by expanding Marx's theory of productive work to include reproductive labor in all its different dimensions, we can not only craft a theory of gender relations in capitalism but gain a new understanding of the class struggle and the means by which capitalism reproduces itself through the creation of different labor regimes and different forms of uneven development and underdevelopment.

Placing the reproduction of labor power at the center of capitalist production unearths a world of social relations that are invisible in Marx but are essential to expose the mechanisms that regulate the exploitation of labor. It discloses that the unpaid labor capital extracts from the working class is far greater than Marx ever imagined, extending to women's domestic work, in addition to the work of those employed on the many plantations that capitalism has constructed in the regions that it has colonized. In all these cases, not only have the forms of work and coercion involved been naturalized, but they have become part of a global assembly line designed to cut the cost of reproducing waged workers. On this line, the unpaid domestic labor ascribed to women as their natural destiny joins with and relays the work of millions of campesinas, subsistence farmers, and informal laborers, growing and producing for a pittance the commodities that waged workers consume or providing at the lowest cost the services their reproduction requires. Hence the hierarchies of labor that so much racist and sexist ideology has tried to justify, but which demonstrate that the capitalist class has been able to maintain its power through a system of indirect rule, delegating to waged workers power over the unwaged, starting with control over the bodies and labor of women.

This means that the wage is not only the terrain of confrontation between labor and capital but also an instrument for the creation of unequal power relations between workers, and that the class struggle is a far more complicated process than Marx assumed. As we have discovered, it must often begin in the family, since to fight capitalism we have had to fight with our husbands and fathers in the same way that black people have had to fight against white workers and the particular type of class composition that capitalism imposes through the wage relation. Last, recognizing that domestic work is labor that (re)produces the workforce enables us to understand gender identities as work functions and gender relations as relations of production, a move that liberates us from the guilt that we have suffered whenever we have wanted to refuse domestic work, and highlights the significance of the feminist principle that "the personal is political."

Why did Marx overlook that part of reproductive work that is most essential for the production of labor power? Elsewhere, I have suggested that the conditions of the working class in England in his time may provide an explanation.[24] When Marx was writing *Capital*, very little housework was performed in the working-class family (as Marx himself recognized), since women were employed side by side with men in the factories from dawn to sunset. Housework, as a branch of capitalist production, was below Marx's historical and political horizon. Only in the latter half of the nineteenth century, after two decades of working-class revolts in which the specter of communism haunted Europe, did the capitalist class begin to invest in the reproduction of labor power, in conjunction with a shift in the form of accumulation, from light (textile-based) to heavy (coal, steel-based) industry, requiring a more intensive labor discipline and a less emaciated workforce. As I wrote in a recent essay, "In Marxian terms, we can say that the development of reproductive work and the consequent emergence of the full-time proletarian housewife were in part the products of the transition from 'absolute' to 'relative surplus' value extraction as a mode of exploitation of labor."[25] They were the product of a shift from a system of exploitation based on the absolute lengthening of the workday to one in which its reduction would be compensated by a technological revolution intensifying the rate of exploitation. A key factor in the change was the capitalists' fear that the super-exploitation to which workers were subjected due to the absolute extension of the workday and meager wages was leading to the extinction of the working class and to women's refusal of housework and childcare—a frequent theme in the official reports that the English government ordered starting in the 1840s to assess the factory worker's living conditions and state of health.[26] It was at this juncture that labor reform was introduced, through a series of Factory Acts that first reduced and then eliminated women's factory employment and substantially increased the male wage (by 40 percent by the end of the century).[27]

The wretched state of the industrial proletariat, which Engels powerfully portrayed in *The Condition of the Working Class in England* (1845), partly explains why housework is almost nonexistent in Marx's work. It is likely, however, that Marx also ignored domestic labor because it lacked the characteristics that in his view defined work under capitalism, which he identified with waged industrial labor. Being home-based, organized in a noncooperative manner, and performed at a low level of technological development, even in the twentieth century, housework has continued to be classified by Marxists as a vestigial element of an older form of productions. As Dolores Hayden pointed out in *The Grand Domestic Revolution*,[28] even when they called for socialized domestic work, socialist thinkers did not believe it could ever be meaningful work,[29] and, like August Bebel, they envisioned a time when housework would be reduced to a minimum.[30]

It took a women's revolt against housework in the 1960s and 1970s to prove that domestic work is "socially necessary labor" in the capitalist sense;[31] that, although it is not organized on an industrial basis, it is extremely productive,[32] and that, to a great extent, it is work that cannot be mechanized; reproducing the individuals in which labor power subsists requires a variety of emotional, as well as physical, services that are interactive in nature and, therefore, very labor-intensive.

This realization has further destabilized Marx's theoretical and political framework, forcing us to rethink one of its main tenets, which is that with the development of capitalism most necessary labor will be industrialized and automated, and, most important, that capitalist and large-scale industry create the material conditions for the construction of a nonexploitative society.

Machinery, Modern Industry, and Reproduction

Marx presumed that capitalism and modern industry must set the stage for the advent of communism, because he believed that without a leap in the productivity of work humanity would be condemned to an endless conflict motivated by scarcity, destitution, and competition for the necessities of life.[33] He also viewed modern industry as the embodiment of a higher rationality, making its way into the world with sordid motives but teaching human beings attitudes apt to develop our capacities to the fullest, as well as liberating us from work. Modern industry is for Marx not only the means to a reduction of "socially necessary labor" but the very model of work, teaching workers uniformity, regularity, and the principles of technological development, thereby enabling us to engage, interchangeably, in different kinds of labor,[34] something, he reminds us, the detailed worker of manufacture, and even the artisan tied to the métier, could never achieve.

Capitalism, in this context, is the rough hand that brings large-scale industry into existence, clearing the way for the concentration of the means of production and cooperation in the work process, developments that Marx considered essential for the expansion of the productive forces and an increase in the productivity of work. For him, capitalism is also the whip that educates human beings in the requirements of self-government, like the necessity to produce beyond subsistence and the capacity for social cooperation on a large scale.[35] Class struggle plays an important role in this process. Workers' resistance to exploitation forces the capitalist class to revolutionize production in such a way as to further economize labor in a sort of mutual conditioning, continually reducing the role of work in the production of wealth, and replacing with machines the tasks that human beings have historically tried to escape. Marx believed that once this process was completed, once modern industry reduced socially necessary labor to a minimum, an era would begin in which we would finally become the masters of our existence and of our natural environment and would not only be able to satisfy our needs but would also be free to dedicate our time to higher pursuits.

How this rupture would occur he did not explain, except through a set of metaphoric images suggesting that, once fully developed, the forces of production would break the shell enveloping them triggering a social revolution. Again, he did not clarify how we would recognize when the forces of production would be mature enough for revolution, only suggesting that the turning point would come with the worldwide extension of capitalist relations, when the homogenization and universalization of the forces of production and the correspondent capacities in the proletariat would reach a global dimension.[36]

This vision of a world in which human beings can use machines to free themselves from want and toil, with free time becoming the measure of wealth, has exercised an immense attraction. André Gorz's image of a postindustrial and work-free society where people dedicate themselves to their self-development owes much to it.[37] Witness also the fascination among Italian autonomist Marxists with the "Fragment on Machines" in the *Grundrisse*, the text in which this vision is most boldly presented. Antonio Negri in particular, in *Marx beyond Marx* (1991), has singled it out as the most revolutionary aspect of Marx's theory. Indeed, the pages of "Notebook VI" and "Notebook VII," where Marx describes a world in which the law of value has ceased to function, as science and technology have eliminated living labor from the production process, and the workers only act as the machines' supervisors, are breathtaking in their anticipatory power.[38] Yet we are today in a good position to see how illusory are the powers that an automated system of production can place at our disposal. We can see that "the allegedly highly productive industrial system" that Marx so much admired "has been in reality a parasite on the earth, the likes of which have never been seen in the history of humanity,[39] and it is now consuming it at a velocity that casts a long shadow over the future. Ahead of his time in recognizing the interplay of humanity and nature, as Ariel Salleh has noted,[40] Marx intuited this process, observing that the industrialization of agriculture depletes the soil as much as it depletes the worker.[41] However, he obviously believed that this trend could be reversed, that once taken over by the workers the means of production could be redirected to serve positive objectives, and that the demise of capitalism was so imminent as to limit the damage a profit-bound industrialization would inflict on the earth.

On all these counts he was deeply mistaken. Machines are not produced by machines in a sort of immaculate conception. Taking the computer as an example, we see that even this most common machine is an ecological disaster, requiring tons of soil and water for its production.[42] Multiplied by the order of billions, we must conclude that, like sheep in sixteenth-century England, machines today are "eating the earth" at such a rapid rate that even if a revolution were to take place in the near future, the work required to make this planet habitable again would be astounding.[43] Machines, moreover, require a material and cultural infrastructure that affects not only our natural commons—lands, woods, waters, mountains, seas, rivers, and coastlines—but our psyche and social relations, molding subjectivities, creating new needs and habits, producing dependencies that also place a mortgage on the future. This partly explains why, a century and a half after the publication of *Capital*, vol. i, capitalism gives no sign of dissolving, though the objective conditions that Marx envisioned as necessary for social revolution seem more than mature.

What we witness, instead, is a regime of permanent primitive accumulation reminiscent of the sixteenth-century enclosures, this time organized by the International Monetary Fund and the World Bank, with a cohort of mining and agribusiness companies that are privatizing communal lands in Africa, Asia, and Latin America and expropriating small-scale producers to acquire the lithium, coltan, and diamonds modern industry requires.[44] We must also stress that none of the means of production that capitalism has developed can be unproblematically taken over and applied to a different use. In the same way as we cannot take over the state, we cannot take over capitalist industry, science, and technology, as the exploitative objectives for which they were created shape their constitution and mode of operation.

That modern industry and technology cannot simply be appropriated and reprogrammed for different purposes is best demonstrated by the growth of the nuclear and chemical industries, which have poisoned the planet and provided the capitalist class with an immense arsenal of weapons now threatening us with annihilation or, at the very least, with the mutual destruction of the contending classes. As Otto Ullrich has put it, "the most outstanding achievement of a scientized technology has been to increase the destructive power of the war machine."[45] Similarly, the allegedly rational industrial management of agriculture, which Marx contrasted to the presumably irrational method of cultivation of small producers,[46] has destroyed the abundance, diversity, and value of food, and much of it will have to be discarded in a society where production is for human beings rather than being an instrument of capital accumulation.

There is another consideration that makes us question Marx's concept of the function of technology in the formation of a communist society, especially when examined from a feminist point of view. A machine-based communism relies on an organization of work that excludes the most basic activities human beings perform on this planet. As I have mentioned, the reproductive work that Marx's analysis bypasses is, to a large extent, work that cannot be mechanized. In other words, Marx's vision of a society in which necessary labor can be drastically reduced through automation clashes with the fact that the largest amount of work on earth is of a highly relational nature and hardly subject to mechanization. Ideally, in a postcapitalist society, we would mechanize several household chores, and we would rely on new forms of communication for learning, amusement, information, once we controlled what technology is produced, for what purposes, and under what conditions. But how can we mechanize washing, cuddling, consoling, dressing and feeding a child, providing sexual services, or assisting those who are ill and the elderly and not self-sufficient? What machine could incorporate the skills and affects needed for these tasks? Attempts have been made, with the creation of *nursebots*,[47] as well as interactive *lovebots*, and it is possible that in the future we may see the production of mechanical mothers. But even assuming that we could afford such devices, we must wonder at what emotional cost we would introduce them into our homes to replace living labor. If, on the other hand, reproductive work can only be partially mechanized, then the Marxian scheme that makes the expansion of material wealth dependent on automation and the reduction of necessary labor implodes; since domestic work, especially the care of children, constitutes most of the work on this planet. The very concept of socially necessary labor loses much of its cogency. How is socially necessary labor to be defined if the largest and most indispensable sector of work on the planet is not recognized as essential? By what criteria and principles will the organization of care work, sexual work, and procreation be governed if these activities are not considered part of socially necessary labor?

The increasing skepticism about the possibility of substantially reducing domestic work through mechanization is one of the reasons why there is now among feminists a renewed interest and experimentation with more collective forms of reproduction and the creation of reproductive commons,[48] allowing for the redistribution of work among a larger number of subjects than the nuclear family provides.[49] Meanwhile, under the pressure of the economic crisis, struggles in defense of our natural commons (lands, waters, forests) and the creation of communing activities (e.g., collective shopping and cooking, urban gardening) are multiplying. It is also significant that "the bulk of the world's daily needs continue to be supplied by Third World women food growers working outside the cash nexus" and with very limited technological inputs, often farming on unused public land.[50] At a time of genocidal austerity programs, the work of these female farmers makes the difference between life and death for millions.[51] Yet this is the very type of subsistence-oriented work that Marx believed should be eliminated, as he considered the rationalization of agriculture—that is, its organization on a large scale and on a scientific basis—"one of the great merits of the capitalist mode of production" and argued that this was possible only through the expropriation of the direct producer.[52]

On the Myth of the Progressiveness of Capitalism

While a critique of Marx's theory concerning the power of industrialization to free humanity from toil and want is in order, there are other reasons his belief in the necessity for and progressiveness of capitalism must be rejected. First, this theory underestimates the knowledge and wealth produced by noncapitalist societies and the extent to which capitalism has built its power through their appropriation—a key consideration if we are not to be mesmerized by the capitalist advancement of knowledge and paralyzed in our will to exit from it. Indeed, it is politically important to recall that the societies capitalism destroyed achieved high levels of knowledge and technology thousands of years before the advent of mechanization, learning to navigate the seas across vast expanses of water, discovering by night watches the main astral constellations, and creating the crops that have sustained human life on the planet.[53] Witness the fantastic diversity of seeds and plants that the Native American populations were able to develop, reaching a mastery in agricultural technology so far unsurpassed, with more than two hundred varieties of corn and potatoes created in Mesoamerica alone—a stark contrast to the destruction of diversity we witness at the hands of the scientifically organized capitalist agriculture of our time.[54]

Capitalism did not invent social cooperation or large-scale intercourse, as Marx called trade and cultural exchanges. On the contrary, the advent of capitalism destroyed societies that had been tied by communal property relations and cooperative forms of work, as well as to large trade networks. Highly cooperative work systems were the norm prior to colonization, from the Indian Ocean to the Andes. We can recall the *ayllu* system in Bolivia and Peru and the communal land systems of Africa that have survived into the twenty-first century, all counterpoints to Marx's view concerning the "isolation of rural life."[55] In Europe as well, capitalism destroyed a society of commons, materially grounded not only in the collective use of land and collective work relations but in the daily struggle against feudal power, which created new cooperative forms of life, such as those experimented with by the heretic movements (Cathars, Waldensians) that I analyzed in *Caliban and the Witch*.[56]

Not accidentally, capitalism could only prevail with a maximum of violence and destruction, including the extermination of thousands of women through two centuries of witch-hunts, which broke a resistance that by the sixteenth century had taken the form of peasant wars. Far from being a carrier of progress, the development of capitalism was a counter-revolution that subverted the rise of new forms of communalism produced in the struggle, as well as those existing on the feudal manors on the basis of the shared use of the commons. In addition, much more than the development of large-scale industry is needed to create the revolutionary combination and association of free producers that Marx envisioned at the end of *Capital*, vol. 1.[57] Capital and large-scale industry may boost the "concentration of the means of production" and the cooperation in the work process that results from the division of labor,[58] but the cooperation required for a revolutionary process is qualitatively different from the technical factor that Marx describes as being, along with science and technology, the "fundamental form of the capitalist mode of production."[59] It is even questionable whether we can speak of cooperation with regard to work relations that are not controlled by the workers themselves and, therefore, produce no independent decision-making except at the moment of resistance, when the capitalist organization of the work process is subverted. We also cannot ignore that the cooperation that Marx admired as the mark of the capitalist organization of work historically became possible precisely on the basis of the destruction of workers' skills and their cooperation in struggle.[60]

Second, to assume that capitalist development was inevitable, not to mention necessary or desirable, at any time in history, past or present, is to place ourselves on the other side of people's struggles to resist it. Can we say that the heretics, the Anabaptists, the Diggers, the Maroons, and all the rebel subjects who resisted the enclosure of their commons or fought to construct an egalitarian social order, writing, like Thomas Muntzer, *"omnia sunt communia"* ("all property should be held in common") on their banners, were on the wrong side of history, viewed from the perspective of human liberation? This is not an idle question. For the extension of capitalist relations is not a thing of the past but an ongoing process, still requiring blood and fire, and still generating an immense resistance, which undoubtedly is putting a brake on the capitalist subsumption of every form of production on earth and the extension of waged labor.

To posit capitalism as necessary and progressive is also to underestimate a fact on which I have insisted throughout this chapter: capitalist development is not, or is not primarily, the development of human capacities and above all the capacity for social cooperation, as Marx argued. It is the development of unequal power relations, hierarchies, and divisions, which, in turn, generate ideologies, interests, and subjectivities that constitute a destructive social force. Not accidentally, in the face of the most concerted neoliberal drive to privatize the remaining communal and public resources, it is not the most industrialized but the most cohesive communities that are able to resist and, in some cases, reverse the privatization tide. As the struggles of indigenous people have demonstrated—the struggle of the Quechua and Aymara against the privatization of water in Bolivia,[61] the struggles of the U'wa people in Colombia against the destruction of their lands by oil drilling, among other examples—it is not where capitalist development is at its highest point but where communal bonds are the strongest that capitalist expansion is halted and even forced to recede. Indeed, as the prospect of a world revolution fueled by capitalist development recedes, the reconstitution of communities devastated by racist and sexist policies and multiple rounds of enclosure appears not just an objective condition but a precondition for social change.

From Communism to the Commons, a Feminist Perspective

Opposing the divisions that capitalism has created on the basis of race, gender, and age, reuniting what has been separated in our lives and reconstituting a collective interest must then be a political priority for feminists and other social justice movements today. This is what is ultimately at stake in the politics of the commons, which, at its best, presupposes a sharing of wealth, collective decision-making, and a revolution in our relationship with ourselves and others. The social cooperation and knowledge-building that Marx attributed to industrial work can be constructed only through communing activities—urban gardening, time-banking, open-sourcing—that are self-organized and both require and produce community. In this sense, insofar as it aims to reproduce our lives in ways that strengthen mutual bonds and set limits to capital accumulation,[62] the politics of the commons partially translates Marx's idea of communism as the abolition of the present state of things. It can also be argued that with the development of online commons—the rise of the free software, free culture movements—we are now approximating that universalization of human capacities that Marx anticipated as a result of the development of productive forces. Nonetheless, the politics of the commons is a radical departure from what communism has signified in the Marxist tradition and in much of Marx's work, starting with the *Communist Manifesto*. There are several crucial differences between the politics of the commons and communism that stand out, especially if we consider these political forms from a feminist and ecological point of view.

Commons, as discussed by feminist writers like Vandana Shiva, Maria Mies, and Ariel Salleh and practiced by grassroots women's organizations, do not depend for their realization on the development of the productive forces, on the mechanization of production, or on any global extension of capitalist relations—the preconditions for Marx's communist project. On the contrary, they contend with the threats posed to them by capitalist development and revalorize locale-specific knowledges and technologies.[63] They do not assume that there is a necessary connection between scientific/technological and moral/intellectual development, which is a central premise of Marx's conception of social wealth. They also place the restructuring of reproduction, as the crucial terrain for the transformation of social relations, at the center of their political project, thus subverting the value structure of the capitalist organization of work. In particular, they attempt to break down the isolation that has characterized domestic work in capitalism, not in view of its reorganization on an industrial scale but to create more cooperative forms of care work.

Commons are declined in the plural, in the spirit promoted by the Zapatistas, with the slogan "One No, Many Yeses," which recognizes the existence of diverse historical and cultural trajectories and the multiplicity of social outcomes that are compatible with the abolition of exploitation. While it is recognized that the circulation of ideas and technological know-how can be a positive historical force, the prospect of a universalization of knowledge, institutions, and forms of behavior is increasingly opposed not only as a colonial legacy but as a project achievable only through the destruction of local lives and cultures. Above all, commons do not depend for their existence on a supporting state. Though in radical circles there is still a lingering desire for the state as a transitional form, presumably required to eradicate entrenched capitalist interests and administer those elements of the commonwealth that demand large-scale planning (water, electricity, transport services, etc.), the state form is today in crisis, and not only in feminist and other radical circles. Indeed, the popularity of the politics of the commons is directly related to the crisis of the state form, which the failure of realized socialism and the internationalization of capital has made dramatically evident. As John Holloway put it in *Change the World without Taking Power*, to imagine that we can use the state to bring forth a more just world is to attribute to it an autonomous existence, abstract from its network of social relations that inextricably tie it to capital accumulation and compel it to reproduce social conflict and mechanisms of exclusion. It is also to ignore the fact "that capitalist social relations have never been limited by state frontiers" but are globally constituted.[64] Moreover, with a world proletariat divided by gender and racial hierarchies, the "dictatorship of the proletariat" concretized in a state form would risk becoming the dictatorship of the white / male sector of the working class. Those with more social power might very well steer the revolutionary process toward objectives that maintain the privileges they have acquired.

After decades of betrayed expectations and electoral ballots, there is now a profound desire, especially among younger people in every country to reclaim the power to transform our lives, reclaim the knowledge and responsibility that in a proletarian state we would alienate to an overarching institution that, in representing us, would replace us. This would be a disastrous turn. For rather than creating a new world we would forfeit that process of self-transformation without which no new society is possible and reconstitute the very conditions that today make us passive even in the face of the most egregious cases of institutional injustice. It is one of the attractions of the commons as the "embryonic form of a new society" that it stands for a power that comes from the ground rather than from the state and relies on cooperation and collective forms of decision-making rather than coercion.[65] In this sense, the spirit of the commons resonates with Audre Lorde's insight that "the master's tools will never dismantle the master's house,"[66] and I believe that if Marx lived today he would agree with that. For though he did not much dwell on the ravages produced by the capitalist organization of sexism and racism, and he gave scarce attention to the transformation in the subjectivity of the proletariat, he nevertheless understood that we need a revolution to liberate ourselves not only from external constraints but from the internalization of capitalist ideology and relations, from, as he put it, "all the muck of ages," so that we become "fitted to found society anew."[67]

Notes

1   "Marx, Feminism, and the Construction of the Commons" was originally published in Shannon Brincat, ed., *Communism in the 21st Century, Volume 1, The Father of Communism: Rediscovering Marx's Ideas* (Oxford: Praeger, 2014). It was later republished in Silvia Federici, *Re-enchanting the World: Feminism and the Politics of the Commons* (Oakland: PM Press, 2019).

2   Karl Marx and Frederick Engels, *The German Ideology*, part 1 (New York: International Publishers, 1988 [1932]), 56–57.

3   Heidi I. Hartmann, "The Unhappy Marriage of Marxism and Feminism: Towards a More Progressive Union," *Capital and Class* 3, no. 2 (Summer 1979): 1–33.

4   This argument is based on readings of Marx's *Ethnological Notebooks*, notes Marx collected in the last years of his life in preparation for a major work on the topic. His comments here show that Lewis Henry Morgan's *Ancient Society* "especially its detailed account of the Iroquois, for the first time gave Marx insights into the concrete possibilities of a free society as it had actually existed in history," and the possibility of a revolutionary path not dependent on the development of capitalist relations. Rosemont argues that Morgan was on Marx's mind when, in correspondence with Russian revolutionaries, he considered the possibility of a revolutionary process in Russia moving directly to communal forms of ownership on the basis of the Russian peasant commune rather than through its dissolution; see Franklin Rosemont, "Karl Marx and the Iroquois," in *Arsenal: Surrealist Subversion* (Chicago: Black Swan Press, 1989), 201–13;

also see Kevin B. Anderson, "Marx's Late Writings on Non-Western and Precapitalist Societies and Gender," *Rethinking Marxism* 14, no. 4 (Winter 2002): 84–96; T. Shanin, *Late Marx and the Russian Road: Marx and the "Peripheries" of Capitalism* (New York: Monthly Review Press, 1983), 29–31.

5   Antonio Negri, for instance, has claimed that the *Grundrisse* should be seen as the culmination of Marx's thought, and that the importance of *Capital* has been overestimated, for it is in the *Grundrisse* that Marx developed his major concepts and his most radical definition of communism; see Antonio Negri, *Marx beyond Marx: Lessons on the Grundrisse*, ed. Jim Fleming, trans. Harry Cleaver (New York: Autonomedia, 1991), 5–4, 8–9, 11–18. By contrast, George Caffentzis argues that *Capital* has a more integrative concept of capitalism and, in this later work, Marx discarded some of the main theses in the *Grundrisse*, like the thesis that capitalism, through the automation of production, can go beyond the law of value; see George Caffentzis, "From the *Grundrisse* to *Capital* and Beyond: Then and Now," *Workplace: A Journal for Academic Labor* no. 15 (September 2008): 59–74.

6   Ariel Salleh, *Ecofeminism as Politics: Nature, Marx and the Postmodern* (London: Zed Books, 1997), 71; Bertell Ollman, *Dialectical Investigations* (New York: Routledge, 1993).

7   Stevi Jackson, "Why a Materialist Feminism Is (Still) Possible," *Women's Studies International Forum* 24, nos. 3–4 (2001): 284.

8   Negri, *Marx beyond Marx*.

9   As Frantz Fanon wrote in *The Wretched of the Earth*: "This is why Marxist analysis should always be slightly stretched every time we have to do with the colonial problem. Everything up to and including the very nature of society, so well explained by Marx, must here be thought out again"; Frantz Fanon, *The Wretched of the Earth* (New York: Grove, 1986 [1961]), 40.

10   Roderick Thurton, "Marxism in the Caribbean," in *Two Lectures by Roderick Thurton: A Second Memorial Pamphlet* (New York: George Caffentzis and Silvia Federici, 2000).

11   On this subject, see W.E.B. Du Bois, "Marxism and the Negro Problem," *The Crisis* (May 1933): 103, 104, 108; also see Cedric Robinson, *Black Marxism: The Making of the Black Radical Tradition* (Chapel Hill: North Carolina University Press, 1983).

12   Joel Kovel argues that Marx remained a prisoner of a scientistic and productivist viewpoint, postulating "a passive nature worked over by an active Man" and encouraging the "all-out development of the productive forces"; Joel Kovel, "On Marx and Ecology," *Capitalism, Nature, Socialism* 22, no. 1 (September 2011): 13, 15. There is, however, a broad debate on the subject to which I can only cursorily refer; see, for instance, John Bellamy Foster, "Marx and the Environment," *Monthly Review* 47, no. 2 (July 1995): 108–23; John Bellamy Foster and Brett Clark, *The Robbery of Nature* (New York: Monthly Review Press, 2020).

13   Roman Rosdoldsky, The Making of Marx's "Capital" (London: Pluto Press, 1977); Negri, *Marx beyond Marx*.

14 Mariarosa Dalla Costa, "Women and the Subversion of the Community,"
    in *The Power of Women and the Subversion of the Community*, ed. Selma
    James and Mariarosa Dalla Costa (Bristol: Falling Wall Press, 1975); Selma
    James, *Sex, Race and Class* (Bristol: Falling Wall Press, 1975); Leopoldina
    Fortunati, *The Arcane of Reproduction: Housework, Prostitution, Labor and
    Capital* (Brooklyn: Autonomedia, 1995).

15 Maria Mies, *Patriarchy and Accumulation on a World Scale* (London: Zed
    Books, 1986); Ariel Salleh, *Ecofeminism as Politics* (London: Zed Books,
    1997).

16 As Marx writes, "the value of labour-power is determined, as in the
    case of every other commodity, by the labour-time necessary for the
    production, and consequently, also the reproduction of this specific
    article. In so far as it has value, it represents no more than a definite
    quantity of the average social labor objectified in it. Labour-power exists
    only as a capacity of the living individual. Its production consequently
    presupposes his existence. Given the existence of the individual, the
    production of labour-power consists in his reproduction of himself or
    his maintenance"; Karl Marx, *Capital*, vol. 1 (London: Penguin, 1990), 274.

17 Karl Marx, *A Contribution to the Critique of Political Economy*, ed. Maurice
    Dobb (New York: International Publishers, 1989 [1859]), 197.

18 Marx and Engels, *The German Ideology*, 51.

19 Ibid., 52.

20 Commenting on the growing substitution of female for male (workers),
    resulting from the introduction of machinery in the factory, "throw-
    ing every member of the family onto the labor market," Marx writes:
    "Since certain family functions, such as nursing and suckling children,
    cannot be entirely suppressed, the mothers who have been confiscated
    by capital must try substitutes of some sort. Domestic work, such as
    sowing and mending, must be replaced by the purchase of ready-made
    articles. Hence the diminished expenditure of labour in the house is
    accompanied by an increased expenditure of money outside. The cost
    of production of the working class family therefore increases"; Marx,
    Capital, vol. 1, 518n39.

    Referring to this passage Leopoldina Fortunati has noted that "Marx
    managed to see housework only when capital destroyed it, and saw it
    through reading government reports which had realized the problems
    posed by the usurpation of housework far earlier"; Fortunati, *The Arcane
    of Reproduction*, 169.

21 For instance, Marx writes that "the natural increase of the workers
    does not satisfy the requirements of the accumulation of capital"; Marx,
    Capital, vol. 1, 794.

22 Hartman, "The Unhappy Marriage," 1.

23 Silvia Federici, *Revolution at Point Zero: Housework, Reproduction, and
    Feminist Struggle*, rev. ed. (Oakland: PM Press, 2020), 38.

24 Federici, "The Reproduction of Labor Power in the New Global
    Economy," in *Revolution at Point Zero*, 104.

25 Here, Federici refers to Marx, *Capital*, vol. 1, chapter 16, part V.

26 Ibid., 348, 591, 630. The last two pages cited discuss the effects of factory employment on women and children's health and women's reproductive work. As Marx put it: "Aside from the daily more threatening advance of the working class movement, the limiting of factory labor was dictated by the same necessity as forced the manuring of English fields with guano. The same blind desire for profit that in one case exhausted the soil had in the other case seized hold of the vital force of the nation at its roots."

27 It is no coincidence that by 1870 we have in England both a new Marriage Act and the Education Act (which introduced the right to universal primary education), both signifying a new level of investment in the reproduction of the workforce. Starting in the same period, hand in hand with the hike in the family wage, we have a change in the eating habits of people in Britain and the means of food distribution, with the appearance of the first neighborhood food shops. In the same period the sewing machine begins to enter the proletarian home; see Eric. I. Hobsbawm, *Industry and Empire: The Making of Modern English Society, 1750 to the Present Day* (New York: Random House, 1968), 135–36, 141.

28 Dolores Hayden, *The Grand Domestic Revolution: A History of Feminist Designs for American Homes, Neighborhoods and Cities* (Cambridge, MA: MIT Press, 1982).

29 Ibid., 6.

30 August Bebel, *Women under Socialism* (New York: Schocken Books, 1971 [1883]).

31 "Socially necessary labour-time is the labour-time required to produce any use value under the conditions of production normal for a given society and with the average degree of skill and intensity of labour prevalent in that society"; Marx, *Capital*, vol. 1, 129.

32 As Leopoldina Fortunati has shown, the waged workers' incorporation of domestic labor allows for their more intense exploitation. It is precisely what makes domestic work different from industrial work—she argues—that accounts for its unique productivity. For the illusion it generates that what wives, mothers, and daughters provide is not work but an expression of love enables workers to treat the home not as place of work but as an escape from the factory, where they can recuperate not only their strength but their dignity, and, as such, it has a pacifying effect; Leopoldina Fortunati, *The Arcane of Reproduction*.

33 Marx and Engels, *The German Ideology*, 56.

34 Marx, *Capital*, vol. 1, 618.

35 Ibid., 775.

36 Marx and Engels, *The German Ideology*, 55ff; Karl Marx and Frederick Engels, *The Communist Manifesto* (Harmondsworth, UK: Penguin Books, 1967 [1848]).

37 André Gorz, *A Farewell to the Working Class* (London: Pluto, 1982); also see André Gorz, *Paths to Paradise: On the Liberation from Work* (London: Pluto, 1985); on this subject, also see Edward Granter, *Critical Social Theory and the End of Work* (Burlington, VT: Ashgate, 2009). Granter points out that

Gorz's idea of a society in which free time is a measure of wealth is a Marxian idea, and, in fact, Gorz makes explicit reference to Marx with quotes from the *Grundrisse*; Granter, *Critical Social Theory*, 121.

38 Negri, *Marx beyond Marx*.

39 Otto Ullrich, "Technology," in *The Development Dictionary: A Guide to Knowledge as Power*, ed. Wolfgang Sachs (London: Zed Books, 1993), 281.

40 Salleh, *Ecofeminism as Politics*, 70.

41 As Marx wrote: "all progress in capitalist agriculture is a progress in the art, not only of robbing the worker, but of robbing the soil; all progress in increasing the fertility of the soil for a given time is a progress towards ruining the more long-lasting sources of that fertility. The more a country proceeds from large-scale industry as the background of its development, as in the case of the United States, the more rapid is this process of destruction. Capitalist production, therefore, only develops the techniques and the degree of combination of the social process of production by simultaneously undermining the original sources of all wealth—the soil and the worker"; Marx, *Capital*, vol. 1, 638.

42 Saral Sarkar, *Eco-Socialism or Eco-Capitalism? A Critical Analysis of Humanity's Fundamental Choices* (London: Zed Books, 1999), 126–27.

43 Think, for example, of the work necessary to monitor and neutralize the damaging effects of the nuclear waste piles accumulated across the globe.

44 See Silvia Federici, "War Globalization and Reproduction," in *Revolution at Point Zero*, 86–94; Silvia Federici, "Women, Land Struggles, and the Reconstruction of the Commons," *Working USA* 14, no. 1 (March 2011); Silvia Federici, "Witch-Hunting, Globalization, and Feminist Solidarity in Africa Today," *Journal of International Women's Studies* 10, no. 1, (October 2008); republished in Silvia Federici, *Witches, Witch-Hunting, and Women* (Oakland: PM Press, 2018).

45 Ullrich, "Technology," 227.

46 Karl Marx, *Capital*, vol. 3 (London: Penguin, 1991 [1885]), 948–49.

47 Nancy Folbre, "Nursebots to the Rescue? Immigration, Automation, and Care," *Globalizations* 3, no. 3 (September 2006): 356.

48 On this subject, see Silvia Federici, "Feminism and the Politics of the Commons in an Era of Primitive Accumulation," in *Revolution at Point Zero*, 156–66.

49 Exemplary here is "The Grand Domestic Revolution," an ongoing living research project inspired by Dolores Hayden's work and initiated by feminist artists, designers, and activists in Utrecht, Holland, to explore how the domestic sphere, as well as the neighborhoods and the cities, can be transformed and "new forms of living and working in common" can be constructed.

50 Salleh, *Ecofeminism as Politics*, 79; Federici, "Feminism and the Politics of the Commons," 138–48.

51 According to the United Nations Population Fund, in 2001, "some 200 million city dwellers" were growing food "providing about 1 billion people with at least part of their food supply"; United Nations Population

Fund, *State of the World Population 2001* (New York: United Nations, 2001). A 2011 Worldwatch Institute Report of confirms the importance of subsistence farming, noting in a press release: "Currently an estimated 800 million people worldwide are engaged in urban agriculture, producing 15–20 percent"; Worldwatch Institute, "State of the World 2011: Innovations That Nourish the Planet" (press release), June 16, 2011, accessed April 2, 2021, http://www.environmentandsociety.org/mml/state-world-2011-innovations-nourish-planet.

52 Marx, *Capital*, vol. 3, 754–55.

53 Clifford D. Conner, *A People's History of Science: Miners, Midwives, and "Low Mechanicks"* (New York: Nation Books, 2005).

54 Jack Weatherford, *How the Indians of the Americas Transformed the World* (New York: Fawcett Columbine, 1988).

55 See Hal Draper, *The Adventures of the Communist Manifesto* (Berkeley: Center for Socialist History, 1998), paragraph 28.

56 Silvia Federici, *Caliban and the Witch: Women, Body and Primitive Accumulation* (New York: Autonomedia, 2004).

57 Marx, *Capital*, vol. 1, 930n2

58 Ibid., 927.

59 Ibid., 454.

60 On this subject, see Marx, *Capital*, vol. 1, 563–68. In "Machinery and Large-scale Industry," section 5, "The Struggle between Worker and Machine," Marx writes: "The instrument of labor strikes down the worker." Not only do the capitalists use machines to free themselves from dependence on labor but machinery is "the most powerful method for suppressing strikes. . . . It would be possible to write a whole history of the inventions made since 1830 for the sole purpose of providing capital with weapons against working-class revolt"; ibid., 562–63.

61 Raquel Guitiérrez Aguilar, *Los Ritmos del Pachakuti: Levantamiento y Movilizacion En Bolivia (2000–2005)* (Miguel Hidalgo, MX: Sisifo Ediciones, 2009).

62 Massimo de Angelis, *The Beginning of History: Value Struggles and Global Capital* (London: Pluto Press, 2007).

63 Maria Mies and Vandana Shiva, *Ecofeminism* (London: Zed Books, 1986); The Ecologist, *Whose Common Future? Reclaiming the Commons* (Philadelphia: Earthscan, 1993).

64 John Holloway, *Change the World without Taking Power: The Meaning of Revolution Today* (London: Pluto Press, 2002), 14, 95.

65 John Holloway, *Crack Capitalism* (London: Pluto Press, 2010), 29.

66 Audre Lorde, "The Master's Tools Will Never Dismantle the Master's House," in *This Bridge Called My Back: Writings by Radical Women of Color*, eds. Cherríe Moraga and Gloria Anzaldua (New York: Kitchen Table, 1983), 98–101.

67 Marx and Engels, *The German Ideology*, 95.

FIVE

Revolution Begins at Home: Rethinking Marx, Reproduction, and the Class Struggle[1]

Introduction

One reason for the enduring power of Marx's political theory has undoubtedly been his capacity to read the future and anticipate forms of capitalist development that are now unfolding before our eyes in ways that still, 150 years later, make his work a guide for the present. With great intuitional power, Marx anticipated the globalization process, capital's relentless drive to conquer every corner of the world and submit every form of production to the logic of profit and the market. Most important, he anticipated that the internationalization of capital would lead to the formation of not only a global market but also a global accumulation cycle, such that "the division of the world into nation states would lose its economic significance."[2] Similarly, the *Grundrisse*, and especially the "Fragment on Machines,"[3] has been credited with predicting the growing dominance of knowledge and science in the capitalist organization of work, which has led some to postulate the beginning of a new phase of accumulation designated "cognitive capitalism."[4]

In one respect, however, Marx was not ahead of his time. Surprisingly, he did not foresee a development that, in the space of a few decades, would change the composition of the working class and the landscape of the class struggle in Europe and the United States—the formation of a new proletarian family, a process that took place (roughly) between 1860 and World War I, with the gradual exclusion of women and children from factory work, the introduction of the "family wage," and the creation of the proletarian housewife and housework itself as a specific branch of capitalist production, entrusted with the reproduction of the workforce.[5]

With these developments, which inaugurated a new patriarchal regime built on the power of the male wage, a transformation occurred in class relations that escaped Marx's analysis, although in *Capital*, vol. 1, we find many references to the reports of the government-appointed factory inspectors that in England paved the way for this change—the capitalist class was in the process of revolutionizing the proletarian family and gender relations and creating new hierarchies between men and women and new divisions within the proletariat, which cannot be deduced from reading Marx's book. Like Engels, Marx remained anchored to the belief that capitalism destroys the proletarian family and creates the material conditions for more egalitarian gender relations. As they put it in the *Communist Manifesto*:

> The more modern industry becomes developed, the more is the labor of men superseded by that of women. Differences of age and sex have no longer any distinctive social validity for the working class. All are instruments of labor.[6]

Why would Marx—otherwise so futuristic in his analysis of capitalist development—fail to acknowledge that a reorganization of social relations was underway that would restructure male-female relations in England's working-class communities and soon in other countries of Europe and in parts of the United States in a more hierarchical way?

It is one of the theses shaping this essay that Marx did not anticipate or comment upon the restructuring of the proletarian family or the construction of new patriarchal relations within the proletariat, because, according to his political theory, the sphere of familial and gender relations had no specific function in capital accumulation or the constitution of workers' subjectivity and class formation.[7] One consequence of this strategic error has been the rift between the socialist movement and the feminist movement that began to grow in the latter part of the nineteenth century, a rift that has continued almost to the present, to which, as we shall see, Marx contributed as head of the First International. Thus, revisiting Marx's perspective on the family, women's work, and the activities by which our life is reproduced is a way of dialoguing with the present and rethinking the patriarchalism of capital and the left, as well as the conditions for cooperation between Marxism and feminism.

My argument is divided into four parts. In part 1, I examine the evidence and reasons for Marx's undertheorization of "reproduction," focusing on his reductive concept of work and production and his implicit assumption that only waged industrial workers have the power and knowledge to subvert capitalism and create the material conditions for the construction of a communist society. In part 2, I examine Marx's response, as head of the First International, to workers' demands for a policy change with regard to women's labor and family life, confirming his silence with regard to the manifest patriarchalism of sectors of the English male working class. In part 3, I contrast Marx's seemingly neutral stand on the contemporary reorganization of family life with the consequences of this reorganization on social life and class relations, arguing that it was a significant instrument for the cooptation of important sectors of the industrial workforce. Last, in section 4, I reflect on the long-term political consequences of the marginalization of women and reproductive work in the program of both the socialist movement and the Marxist tradition, arguing it is time we ask to what extent this theoretical and political "mistake" affected their organizational capacity and their vision of the society to be built on the ruins of capitalist society.

Marx on Social Reproduction and the Reproduction of Labor Power

A key to understanding the reasons for Marx's failure to acknowledge the momentous changes that were in the making in England, in the nineteenth century, with regard to family life and male-female relations, is his treatment in both *Capital* and the *Grundrisse* of the processes involved in the reproduction of labor power. This should have been a central issue in Marx's political theory, considering the strategic function that labor and labor power play in his analysis of capitalist society and the capitalist organization of work. Labor power for Marx is the engine of capitalist accumulation; it is the substance of value creation, and its exploitation is the terrain on which the struggle for human liberation is decided. Thus, the activities involved in the (re)production of this precious capacity should have had a central place in Marx's theoretical and political framework. But, as we have seen in the previous chapters of this volume, they are scarcely discussed by Marx, and when they are it is in ways that fail to recognize the specific contribution of women's domestic work in this context.

Even when discussing how the workforce is generationally reproduced,[8] Marx is silent on women's role and fails to envisage the possibility of a conflict of interests between women and men and between women and the state with regard to procreation, although for proletarian women a pregnancy was often a death sentence, especially when out of wedlock. Not surprisingly, by the mid–nineteenth century, many were receptive to the campaign that advocates of contraception were conducting within the workers' movement.[9] Apparently oblivious to the high cost of procreation for women, to the anguish that many would experience with every unwanted pregnancy, and the often deadly efforts they would make to abort, Marx speaks of the "natural increase of the population." He also argues that "the capitalist may safely leave this [procreation] to the workers' drives for self-preservation and propagation,"[10] and, in his otherwise trenchant critique of Malthus's population theory, he suggests that capitalism does not depend on women's procreative capacity for the expansion of the workforce, since it can presumably satisfy its labor-needs by means of constant technological revolutions periodically creating a "surplus population."[11] In reality, as a system that makes of labor power the substance of value creation, capitalism has been extremely interested in demographic shifts and has strictly regulated women's reproductive capacity, imposing heavy penalties on their tampering with it,[12] penalties that were in force in most of Europe in Marx's time.[13] Indeed, the capitalist class has never relied exclusively on changes in the organization of production for the creation of a surplus population and the determination of an optimally sized workforce. Marx himself acknowledged that the rate at which industrial capital was consuming workers' lives was such that new recruits, drawn primarily from the rural areas and the employment of women and children, were constantly needed. And he was certainly aware of the concern that the high rates of infant mortality in the industrial districts were generating among the elite. Even in the twentieth century, despite continuous technological revolutions, capitalism has relied on the regulation of women's bodies and on migratory movements to satisfy its need for the quantity and quality of labor power that developing the productive forces and breaking down workers' resistance to exploitation has required.[14]

As with domestic work, the work involved in the activities by which the new generation of workers are produced are not part of Marx's discussion of the capitalist organization of work and exploitation. Thus, absent from his analysis of capitalism is a discussion of a field of activities and forces—affective relations, sexual desires, practices concerning housework and procreation—that previous socialist thinkers had recognized as having a political potential. In Marx, sexual passion and procreation fall outside or remain at the margins of the world of capital's economic relations and workers' decision-making and struggle. Mothering is only mentioned with reference to the female workers' neglect of their children. The prostitute too is invisible as a worker and as a political subject. In Sheila Rowbotham's words, "She appears as an indication of the state of society, not as [a member of] a social group in movement, developing consciousness in history."[15] Pictured as a victim of poverty and moral degradation, she is described as part of that lumpenproletariat that, in *The 18th Brumaire of Louis Bonaparte*, Marx dismissed as "the "refuse of all classes."[16] Marx's view of female factory workers is also reductive. We see their suffering bodies, the inequities to which they were subjected, but we are not told how women's entrance into the factories transformed their subjectivity, changed their relations with men, whether it enhanced or diminished their capacity for struggle, and in what ways their demands differed from men's. With the exception of occasional comments on the degrading impact of industrial and agricultural work on women and girls' "moral character"—due to overwork and exposure to promiscuous work conditions—Marx does not discuss the conduct of female workers. In *Capital*, they remain shadow figures, only represented as victims of abuse, an image in stark contrast with that projected by contemporary political reformers who pictured them—especially when single and not burdened with children—as enjoying a new sense of freedom, thanks to having a wage, leaving home at an early age "to be their own mistresses," and behaving like men.[17]

From the Manifold of Work to Wage Labor and "Production"

Accounting for these silences, questioning why Marx did not extend his critique of political economy to "a detailed examination of social reproduction in the household," John Bellamy Foster has argued that in *Capital* Marx was concerned with providing a critique of capitalism articulated "from the standpoint of its own ideal conception," i.e., "in terms of its inner logic" and, from this viewpoint, reproductive work fell outside the boundaries of value creation.[18] Marx, Bellamy Foster writes, "moved more and more towards embracing the contradictions of the inner and outer determination of capital as a system." That is, he embraced the capitalist obliteration of unpaid reproductive labor, and here—it seems to me—lies the problem. In so doing, he failed to unmask the very presuppositions of classic political economy. Instead of revealing unpaid reproductive work as the source, indeed the "secret," of the reproduction of labor power, he codified the separation between production and reproduction typical of the logic and history of capitalist development and the naturalization of the latter as "women's labor." Significantly, he relegated the only references to domestic work to be found in the three volumes of *Capital* to footnotes.[19]

Arguing in defense of Marx that there is a difference between the exploitation of labor power and the expropriation of the conditions of its production, including women's work and nature,[20] will not do, given Marx's contention that all activities that produce labor power are an essential part of capitalist production.[21]

More is needed to explain why, writing in the midst of a governmental program aiming to reorganize factory and family life, accompanied by choruses of complaints denouncing the collapse of the proletarian family and women's reproductive work, Marx ignored it in his analysis of capitalist exploitation.

It helps to know that he was not alone in his reductive interpretation of work and the class struggle. As Federico Tomasello has argued in *L'Inizio del Lavoro* (The Beginning of Work), since 1830, especially in France, a complex social process had developed, whereby both the state and the incipient workers' movement redefined work and the figure of the worker in ways that excluded the wageless and privileged those engaged in industrial work.[22] The historic insurrection of the Parisian proletariat in 1830, which Victor Hugo immortalized in *Les Miserables*, followed one year later by the takeover of the city of Lyon by revolting weavers, triggered a process of "integration" of selected sectors of the rebel workers, the result of which, Tomasello argues, was the emergence of the laborious, honest wage worker as a juridical figure recognized by the state as the carrier of social rights, such as the right to work, and soon to become the foundation of the modern state and all modern constitutions. The election of waged work as a privileged status with regard to social rights and, with it, the beginning of a unitary representation of the world of work and the separation of the *"classes laborieuses"* from the *"classes dangereuses"* also marked, according to Tomasello, the beginning of the labor unions and socialist movements.[23] This would indicate that Marx's exclusionary conception of the working class was not simply the product of a theoretical stand. Rather, it was also the expression of a political operation whereby the interests of a particular sector of workers were prioritized, both in institutional and radical politics, and an image of the worker was constructed that canonized the *ouvrier*, the *"operaio"*—the generally male, white, waged industrial worker—to the exclusion of the world of unwaged subjects capitalism has exploited, such as houseworkers, campesinas, enslaved Africans, and other colonial subjects—an operation that preceded Marx's political engagement, being juridically codified in France by the early 1840s, but which his analysis contributed to consolidating, the more so as it was presented as the result of a scientific study of social reality.

In this process, a world of struggles—in Europe, as well, until the mid–nineteenth century—that expressed proletarian opposition to the growing hegemony of the market—food riots, riots against price fixing, attacks on bakeries, on food shops, against carts bringing grains to the ports to be exported[24]—was also erased from radical politics. These were struggles that saw the unity of a broad population of proletarians whose subsistence basis was being destroyed in the early part of the nineteenth century by the growing commercialization of land and reproduction, such as the subjection of grain prices to market laws.[25] As Ahlrich Meyer writes:

> This class of the laboring poor consisted of beggars and vagabonds, searching for work, day workers in the country, impoverished farmers and share croppers, weavers of the proto-industrial cottage-industry, domestic servants and city-handymen, seasonal migratory workers, railroad construction workers, proletarianized craftworkers, the manufacturing and factory proletariat and, last but not least those that Marx named the *lumpenproletariat*, the dangerous classes, men, women and children in their totality an extensively mobilized class . . . which for the first time, due to the migration processes, also took on a European dimension.[26]

As Meyer points out, "In a cycle of revolts that lasted for almost 100 years," these pauperized masses had to learn that "their survival was no longer secure," for the conditions of their existence were being transformed into the conditions of capital.[27] Thus, with women in the lead, "They made the subsistence question a public affair," responding with a "praxis of social appropriation" to their "violent expropriation and separation" from the means of their reproduction.[28] Meyer concludes that if, in 1848, the specter of communism haunted Europe, this was because a broad spectrum of proletarians refused to be condemned to poverty and hunger and insisted in mass revolts that their right to existence be guaranteed.[29] In his view, it was because of the defeat of these struggles and "the subjection of the poor and working classes to a new form of subsistence" that a reductive concept of work and the worker and "a wage labour theory" could be constructed.[30]

Be that as it may, the reduction of the working class to waged labor has important consequences in Marx's work that compromise the power of his analysis of capitalism. While throughout *Capital* every articulation of capitalist society—money, credit, rent, machinery—is subjected to a minute analysis, constantly re-elaborated over hundreds of pages, we do not find any in-depth analysis of the function and political consequences of differences and inequalities within the proletariat and the simultaneous existence in capitalism of different labor regimes and forms of exploitation. For instance, neither gender nor race appear in Marx's discussion of the social division of labor. Similarly, Marx deplores that, with the rise of industrial work, the male adult worker, the father, becomes "a slave dealer,"[31] selling the work of his wife and children to his employers, but he does not ask how this was possible. He does not tell us that married women in England were not entitled to receive the wages they earned, as they were not considered legal subjects capable of stipulating contractual relations.

Only with the passing of the Marriage Property Act, in 1870, was the medieval coverture system, which erased married women's existence before the law, terminated.[32] So entrenched was the subordination of women to men in England that the popular custom among laborers of ending a marriage by selling their wives at the local market continued into the late nineteenth century, with cases reported as late as 1901 and 1913.[33] This explains why the patriarchal relations that had prevailed in the "put-out-system" did not vanish when cottage work was displaced by industrialization but were reconstituted in the factories, so that, in a first phase at least, production was again structured according to a gender hierarchy, with the father subcontracting the labor of his wife and children or selling their labor together with his own and making a claim to their wages.

Had Marx analyzed the social roots and implications of this patriarchal policy, he would have recognized the existence of a fundamental anomaly in capitalist relations. He would have seen that the condition that he stipulated for the development of wage labor—i.e., "freedom" intended as "ownership of one's body" and capacity to work—was never extended to women. *He would have further realized that the women's rights, which feminists in his time were fighting for, especially with regard to women's position in marriage and the family, were also labor rights,* since "being covered" by their husbands affected their ability to hold a job, to keep their wages, and to participate in the workers' movement, given that the power that men had to restrict their wives' actions certainly limited women's ability to struggle.

The question of patriarchal relations within the working class was of special importance in Marx's time. When Marx was starting to work on *Capital*, the opposition of male workers to women's presence in the factories intensified after an individual system of wages was introduced that gave unmarried women control over their earnings. As Judy Lown reports in *Women and Industrialization*, such a move was met with hostility by workers, resulting in attempts to define female labor as unskilled and confine women to the worst tasks.[34] Trade unions also upheld "the principles of patriarchy," mobilizing for the passing of "protective legislation" and supporting the male workers' demand for a "family wage," enabling them to support a presumably "nonworking wife."[35] By the mid–nineteenth century, the "male breadwinner norm" was a rallying point for working-class organizations.[36] Again, Marx's *Capital* makes no mention of this gendered struggle, though it plausibly undermined workers' unity and threatened women's source of livelihood. Again, all we find in the three volumes is a footnote stating that "the shortening of the hours of labor for women and children was exacted from capital by the adult male workers."[37]

Gender, Labor, and the Family Wage in the First International Workingmen's Association

Were Marx's silences on such crucial matters the product of political expedience? This is a legitimate question, as we know from his correspondence with Engels that Marx always saw his work in *Capital* as directly connected to the politics and debates within the International Workingmen's Association, of which he was a founder and leader.[38] We also know that women's rights were a subject of much debate within the organization, which was so split on this question that it was not until seven months after its foundation that it voted on the eligibility of women as members and two years before a well-known woman, Harriet Law, was placed in a leadership position as a member of the General Council. Yet Marx made no mention of women's special situation in his inaugural speech. According to the record, he "did not made any specific place for working women, whose oppression was apparently considered to be simply part of that of workers."[39] He also campaigned in the early 1870s to expel Section 12 of the IWA, its most feminist wing,[40] which was supporting women's suffrage, "free love," and what its leader Victoria Woodhull referred to as "social freedom," i.e., women's independence from the male wage and the domestic slavery inscribed in marriage.[41] It is worth noting that wage earning was used in the expulsion process, as the General Council of the IWA (largely under the influence of Marx) "inaugurated a 'two-thirds' rule, holding that two-thirds of the members of any IWA section had to be wage laborers, a decision that favored the participation of workers in trades and crafts but largely excluded reform-minded women."[42] This expulsion had a profound impact on the development of the working-class revolutionary movement, possibly as important as the anarchist-communist split that pitted Marx against

Bakunin, as it pushed the questions of gender relations, sexuality, and women's power into the future or, even worse, into the no-go land of bourgeois rights.

As one of International's main spokesmen, Marx undoubtedly knew that the majority of its male members supported a strong limitation of women's factory employment and the institution of a "family wage," and he was likely ambivalent on the matter, in the same way as he was with regard to the destruction of the family in the age of manufacture, which he deplored but also considered instrumental to the liberation of women and children from patriarchal rule.[43] On his "fence-sitting" on the question of the "family wage" we have the testimony of Harriet Law, the only woman member of the General Council of the International. According to Law's protest against his intervention in a debate on this issue, as reported in the minutes of the First International's General Council, Marx had been in favor of women's participation in industrial work, but he had stated that the way in which women and children worked under existing conditions was abominable,[44] thus strengthening the position of the advocates of the family wage.[45] Law believed that Marx had betrayed the interest of working-class women and registered her protest. It is possible, however, that Marx considered the institution of the "family wage" and the reduction of women's factory work a temporary phenomenon, as the progress of industrialization would require women's participation, and, as he wrote in *Capital*, vol. 1, "create a new economic foundation for a higher form of the family and of relations between the sexes."[46]

If this was Marx's assumption in his support for the "family wage," it was a great miscalculation. By the 1870s, an epochal reform program was underway that by the turn of the century transformed class relations and defused class conflict, sending many former female factory workers back to the home and inaugurating a new type of patriarchal regime that can be labeled the "patriarchy of the wage."[47] With these changes the fear of a working-class revolution that had haunted the capitalist class since 1848 was largely dispelled. By the 1880s, in England, as across the Atlantic, a new predominantly male waged workforce emerged that may not have looked at the laws of the capitalist organization of work "as natural laws"—as Marx predicted it would in the course of capitalist development—but was socially and politically domesticated, clearly having new reasons for "feeling at home when not working."[48]

Conclusion

I have argued in this chapter that the limited attention that Marx gave in his major works to such issues as the family, reproductive activities, and gender hierarchies—those that existed in the first phase of industrialization and those that were being constructed in response to the reproductive crisis of the mid–nineteenth century—cannot be attributed solely to the conditions in which working-class families lived during the first phase of the industrial revolution or to a masculinist oversight. Rather, like the contemporary socialist movement, Marx embraced a narrow concept of work and the worker in capitalism, mostly because of his overestimation of the role of capitalist development in the construction of communist society. He also overestimated the power of industrialization to create the material basis for a more egalitarian society and was so convinced that the waged industrial workers were the revolutionary subjects that he was ready to sacrifice to their cause issues and interests that were, in his view, not directly related to the confrontation between capital and labor, such as women's desire for liberation from social and economic dependence from men. Thus, while he may have recognized that the demand for a "family wage" and for restrictions on women's factory work inevitably implied a consolidation of patriarchal relations within the working class, he accepted it, possibly confident that the revolutionary process capitalist development would inevitably spark would redress this situation.

This critique of Marx does not detract from recognizing the powerful contribution he has made to our understanding of capitalist society and (indirectly) to feminist theory. As the recent celebration of the anniversary of the publication of *Capital* have demonstrated, 150 years later, even critics must take Marx's analysis as a point of reference for deciphering the movements of capital and the prospects for its future developments. Whether or not the labor theory of value still describes the process of capital accumulation and whether or not we can explain today's political economy through the falling the rate of profit remain as important questions today as they were at the end of Marx's life, and even now a discussion of social and political relations that does not rely on such concepts as commodification, alienation, and exploitation is hardly imaginable. Feminist theory has also been strengthened by Marx's methodology, which stresses the historically constructed character of social reality and, thereby, rejects naturalized/eternalizing identitarian concepts. Most important, Marx has given us tools to detect capital's reach into the most intimate spheres of our domestic and affective life. But he also underestimated the power of the divisions that capitalism has planted in the body of the proletariat and their consequences for the development of a revolutionary working class.

Highlighting these limits in Marx's work is especially important today, as in the face of the seemingly unlimited destructive powers of capitalist development we must ask why the inevitable revolution that Marx predicted has not taken place. In seeking an answer to this question, it, in fact, helps us to reflect that the Marxist account of capitalist exploitation has until recently ignored the largest sector of work and workers on earth and has excluded from the class struggle a host of issues that are crucial to the lives of workers and their relation to capital and the state. There is no denying that women, domestic work, sex work, and child raising have been absent from Marxist and communist theory and organizing, and that, with rare exceptions, for the Marxist tradition the worker was white and male. A clear example is the way that socialist and communist movements have long dismissed, if not ostracized, concerns that were of the utmost importance for proletarian women and men, for example, birth control. As Wally Seccombe reports, even in the 1910s and 1920s socialist parties opposed the use of contraceptives and limits on the size of families, seeing this as a Malthusian plot "to blame poverty on the poor." Clara Zetkin, for instance, denounced birth control, calling it an "individualistic indulgence" and arguing that "the proletarians must consider the need to have as many fighters as possible."[49] It must be noted, in this context, that it was only in 1891 that the SPD "officially accepted women's equal rights, and then only in a very limited legal sense."[50] Generations of Marxists have also viewed the full-time houseworker as a backward subject incapable of organization. Typically, when, in her 1945 book *In Woman's Defense*, Mary Inman, a Los Angeles factory worker, stressed the productivity of housework, the US Communist Party forbade her from continuing to teach in its school for workers' education.[51] Along similar lines, in the 1960s and 1970s, Marxists proved unable to recognize the importance of the feminist movement and, even more specifically, the feminist struggle against unpaid domestic labor as determinants in the definition of the value of labor power.

Much has changed today in comparison to the 1970s, when feminists were routinely accused of dividing the working class. The development of the student, feminist, and ecological movements, as well as the crisis of waged work, has forced Marxists to look beyond the factory into the school, the environment, and, more recently, "social reproduction" as key terrains for the reproduction of the workforce and working-class struggle. However, with some exceptions, the Marxist left's inability to see the reproduction of human life and labor power and the gender hierarchies built upon it as key elements in the process of accumulation continues. Witness the autonomist Marxists' theorization of the dominance of "immaterial labor" in the present phase of capitalist development, and the associated argument (expanding Marx's vision in the "Fragment on Machines" in the *Grundrisse*) that capitalism is working towards the elimination of living labor from the "production process,"[52] which ignores the fact that reproductive work, especially in the form of childcare, is irreducible to industrialization, and is a paradigmatic example of the interpenetration of emotional and material elements in most forms of work. Witness also the continuing reluctance among many Marxists to criticize Marx's theory that the revolutionary process is premised on the globalization of capitalist production, even though it is now patently clear that this can only occur at the cost of the destruction of the means of reproduction of many populations across the planet. Indeed, should we accept Marx's thesis about capitalism's progressive character, we would have to dismiss some of the most powerful struggles presently taking place across the world as ineffective, if not outright reactionary. For they are clearly struggles against capitalist development, which, in the eyes of indigenous peoples' communities fighting, for instance, against the destruction of their lands and cultures by mining, petroleum drilling, or hydro-electric plants and other "mega projects"—is nothing short of another name for violence.[53]

In conclusion, if the "revolutionary kernel" of Marx's theory is to be rescued from the mountain of developmentalist interpretations and applications under which it has been buried, which Marx undoubtedly inspired, we have to rethink Marxism and capitalism from the viewpoint of the process of reproduction, as some of us have been doing now for four decades, recognizing that this is the most strategic ground both in the struggle against capitalism and for the construction of a nonexploitative society.

Notes

1   "Revolution Begins at Home: Rethinking Marx, Reproduction, and the Class Struggle," was originally published in Marcello Musto, ed., *Marx's Capital After 150 Years: Critiques and Alternatives to Capitalism* (New York: Routledge, 2019).

2   See Luciano Ferrari Bravo, "Vecchie e nuove questioni nella teoria dell'imperialismo," introduction to Luciano Ferrari Bravo, ed., *Imperialismo e classe operaia multinazionale* (Milano: Feltrinelli, 1975), 20–21.

3   Karl Marx, *Grundrisse: Foundations of the Critique of Political Economy* (London: Pelican Books, 1973), 690–710.

4   For advocates of this position, see Michael Hardt and Antonio Negri, *Multitude: War and Democracy in the Age of Empire* (Minneapolis: University of Minnesota Press, 2004); Carlo Vercellone, "From Formal Subsumption to General Intellect: Elements for a Marxist Reading of the Thesis of Cognitive Capitalism," *Historical Materialism* 15, no. 1 (2007):

13–36. For a critique of the concept of "cognitive capitalism," see George Caffentzis, "A Critique of 'Cognitive Capitalism,'" in George Caffentzis, *In Letters of Blood and Fire: Work, Machines, and the Crisis of Capitalism* (Oakland: PM Press, 2013), 95–123.

5   See Wally Seccombe, *Weathering the Storm: Working-Class Families from the Industrial Revolution to the Fertility Decline* (London: Verso, 1993).

6   Karl Marx and Frederick Engels, *The Communist Manifesto* (Harmondsworth, UK: Penguin Books, 1967 [1848]), 88.

7   Ahlrich Meyer, "A Theory of Defeat: Marx and the Evidence of the Nineteenth Century," in Marcel van der Linden and Karl Heinz Roth, eds., *Beyond Marx: Theorising the Global Labor Relations of the Twentieth-First Century* (Leiden, NL: Brill, 2014), 274–76.

8   Marx, *Capital*, vol. 1, 711–24.

9   Notable here was the organizational work of Francis Place, who by 1822 was advocating the use of contraceptive techniques in order for workers to escape a Malthusian fate and begin to control their birthrate. A worker himself, father of fifteen children, Place launched a campaign to advertise his ideas on the matter, circulating handbills addressed to married couples, and later continuing his advocacy after becoming a founder of the Chartist movement. Very popular among workers, especially in the northern districts, Place is considered one of the fathers of the birth control movement. On this issue, see Norman Edwin Himes, *Medical History of Contraception* (New York: Schocken Books, 1970 [1936]).

10 Marx, *Capital*, vol. 1, 718.

11 Marx, *Capital*, vol. 1, 784–85. For a critique of Marx's "surplus population" theory, see Max Henninger "Poverty, Labor, Development: Towards a Critique of Marx's Conceptualizations," in Van der Linden and Roth, *Beyond Marx*, 301–2. He writes: "Much like the reproduction-schemes in *Capital Vol. II*, Marx's theory of relative-surplus population effaces the possibility of autonomous underclass-behaviour and recognizes no other logic but that of capital-valorization."

12 On the relations between the capitalist conception of labor as the essence of value creation and the regulation of women's reproductive capacity, see Silvia Federici, *Caliban and the Witch: Women, Body and Primitive Accumulation* (New York: Autonomedia, 2004), chapter 3, in particular her discussion of the European witch-hunt.

13 In England, an act in 1803 made abortion a statutory crime punishable with whipping, transportation, and even death if the woman was proven quick with child. The statute was reenacted in 1828. Then the Offences Against Persons Act of 1861 established that any person attempting to abort, if convicted, would be punished with penal servitude for life. In every country in Europe, in Marx's time, tampering with procreation was a felony, punishable with many years of imprisonment.

14 For a powerful analysis of state control over birth and fertility rates and its relation to migration policies, see Mariarosa Dalla Costa's "Reproduction and Emigration (1974), published in Mariarosa Dalla Costa, *Women and the Subversion of the Community: A Mariarosa Dalla*

Costa Reader (Oakland: PM Press, 2019), 70–108. Expanding on Mariarosa Dalla Costa's thesis, we can certainly say that it is to women's refusal to carry the burden of producing many children that that we must attribute the formation of a global labor market, as well as the global rise of well-financed, right-wing "pro-life" movements, whose intimidating activities in the United States have been defended by the main legal institution in the country, the Supreme Court.

15 Sheila Rowbotham, *Women, Resistance, and Revolution* (New York: Vintage Books, 1974), 63.

16 Karl Marx, *The 18th Brumaire of Louis Bonaparte* (New York: International Publishers, 1963 [1852]), 75.

17 Ivy Pinchbeck, *Women Workers and the Industrial Revolution: 1750–1850* (New York: F.S. Crofts & Co., 1930), 311–13; also see, e.g., Lord Ashley's intervention during the Parliamentary debates surrounding the Ten Hours Bill of 1847. He complained that the "females not only perform the labor, but occupy the places of men; they are forming various clubs and associations, and are gradually acquiring those privileges that are held to be the proper portion of the male sex"; Judy Lown, *Women and Industrialization: Gender at Work in Nineteenth-Century England* (Minneapolis: University of Minnesota Press, 1990), 44–45, 181.

18 John Bellamy Foster, "Women, Nature and Capital in the Industrial Revolution," *Monthly Review* 69, no. 8 (January 2018): 11.

19 Marx, *Capital*, vol. 1, 517–18n38–39.

20 As evidence, Foster Bellamy quotes a text by Eleanor Marx, in which she speaks of the "expropriation" of women and workers' rights; see John Bellamy Foster, "Women, Nature and Capital in the Industrial Revolution," 12–13.

21 Marx wrote, "Productive labor would therefore be such labour as produces commodities or directly produces, trains, develops, maintains or reproduces labour-power itself"; Karl Marx, *Theories of Surplus Value, Part 1* (Moscow: Progress Publishers, 1969), 172.

22 Federico Tomasello, *L'Inizio del lavoro. Teoria politica e questione sociale nella Francia di prima metá Ottocento* (Roma: Carrocci Editore, 2018), especially 96–98, 105–6.

23 Tomasello stresses the important role of the Sansimonians in the centralization of the figure of the industrial worker and the disappearance from the program of the socialist/working class movement of a series of issues that had been crucial for earlier anti-capitalist struggles, such as "the critique of work and technology, of family and the criminal system"; ibid., 132n38.

24 On the role of women in social protest and collective action in early nineteenth-century England, see Sheila Rowbotham, *Women, Resistance and Revolution*, 102–4.

25 On this subject, see Ahlrich Meyer, "A Theory of Defeat: Marx and the Evidence of the Nineteenth Century," in Van der Linden and Roth, *Beyond Marx*, 258–79.

26 Ibid., 260–61.

27 Ibid., 260.

28 Ibid.

29 Ibid., 261–62.

30 Ibid., 264.

31 As Marx wrote: "Previously the worker sold his own labour-power which he disposed of as a free agent, formally speaking. Now he sells wife and child. He has become a slave-dealer. Notices of demands for children's labour often resemble in form the inquiries for Negro slaves that were formerly read among the advertisements in American journals"; Marx, *Capital*, vol. 1, 519.

32 According to William Blackstone, whose *Commentaries on the Laws of England* systematized English bourgeois legal and judicial practice: "By marriage the very being or legal existence of a woman is suspended, or at least is incorporated or consolidated into that of the husband, under whose wing, protection and cover she performs everything and she is therefore called in our law *'femme covert'"*; see Lee Holocombe, *Wives and Property: Reform of the Married Women's Property Law in Nineteenth-Century England* (Toronto: University of Toronto Press, 1983) 25–26.

33 On the sale of wives, see E.P. Thompson, *Customs in Common: Studies in Traditional Popular Culture* (New York: New Press, 1991). According to Thompson, who has assembled documentation about this practice, the sale or exchange of a wife for sexual or domestic services took place on occasion in most places and at most times, in most parts of England, above all among laborers, such as miners, bakers, chimney sweeps, ironworker, bricklayers, brickmakers, cloth workers, stonecutters, and many other lower-class occupations; Thompson, *Customs in Common*, 408–9, 413–14. Tolerated by the law, the custom was so entrenched that wife sales are recorded even in the first quarter of the twentieth century. In some cases, workhouses forced husbands to sell their wives so as not to have to support them. It was the quickest way, among the lower classes, to end a marriage. Customarily, after parading his wife with a halter around her neck, arm, or waist, a husband would publicly auction her to the highest bidder.

34 Lown, *Women and Industrialization*, 107.

35 Ibid., 213.

36 Seccombe, *Weathering the Storm*, 111–24.

37 Marx, *Capital*, vol. 1, 519n40.

38 On this subject, see William A. Pelz, "'Capital and the First International,'" in Ingo Schmidt and Carlo Fanelli, eds., *Reading "Capital" Today* (London: Pluto Press, 2017), 36–37.

39 See Christine Fauré, *Political and Historical Encyclopedia of Women* (New York: Routledge, 2003), 345–46.

40 Whereas most of sections of the IWA were identified by the section of the production process their largely immigrant German membership were employed in, Section 12 was dominated by US-born radicals (often called "Yankee Internationalists"). As the two factions began sparring, Marx himself recommended the expulsion of the faction that gave

"predominance to the women's question over the question of labor"; see Nancy Folbre, "Socialism, Feminist and Scientific," in Marianne A. Ferber and Julie A. Nelson, eds., *Beyond Economic Man: Feminist Theory and Economics* (Chicago: University of Chicago Press, 2009), 103n. Echoing Marx, a member of Section 1 defended the expulsion: "This nonsense which they talk of, female suffrage and free love, may do to consider in the future, but the question that interests us as working-men is that of labor and wages"; see Amanda Frisken, *Victoria Woodhull's Sexual Revolution: Political Theater and Popular Press in Nineteenth-Century America* (Philadelphia: University of Pennsylvania Press, 2004), 44.

41 As she wrote, "I have heard women reply when this difficulty was pressed upon them, 'We cannot ostracize men as we are compelled to [ostracize] women, since we are dependent on them for support'"; quoted in Frisken, *Victoria Woodhull's Sexual Revolution*, 39.

42 See ibid., 44.

43 Marx, *Capital*, vol. 1, 620.

44 Fauré, *Political and Historical Encyclopedia of Women*, 346.

45 It is interesting, in this context, that one of the few references in Marx's work to a women's struggle is to a wives' mobilization in support of their husbands' demand for a "family wage." As Heather A. Brown reports, in an article written in 1853, Marx, without any comment, described the "efforts by women to ensure that men would be paid a 'family wage,' citing an organizers' argument that every man should have a fair wage, so that 'he could support himself and his family in comfort'"; Heather A. Brown, *Marx on Gender and the Family: A Critical Study*, Historical Materialism 39 (London: Brill, 2012), 103.

46 Marx, *Capital*, vol. 1, 620–21.

47 Federici, *Caliban and the Witch*, especially chapter 3.

48 The reference here is to Marx's discussion of "estranged labor," i.e., the fact that since work in capitalism is for the worker an alienating activity, "[t]he worker therefore only feels himself outside his work, and in his work he feel outside himself, and when he is working he is not at home. He is at home when he is not working. His labour is therefore not voluntary but forced labour"; Karl Marx, *Economic and Philosophical Manuscripts of 1844*, trans. Martin Milligan (Moscow: Foreign Languages Publishing House 1961), 72. This comment has often been criticized by feminists as a further example of his devaluation of reproductive activities.

49 Seccombe, *Weathering the Storm*, 164–66, especially 165.

50 Rowbotham, *Women, Resistance, and Revolution*, 80.

51 On this history, see Kate Weigand, *Red Feminism: American Communism and the Making of Women's Liberation* (Baltimore: Johns Hopkins University Press, 2001).

52 Marx, *Capital*, vol. 1, 690–710.

53 See Naomi Klein, *This Changes Everything: Capitalism vs. the Climate* (New York: Simon and Schuster, 2014).

The Construction of Domestic Work in Nineteenth-Century England and the Patriarchy of the Wage[1]

To this day, domestic work is considered by many to be women's natural vocation, so much so that it is often labeled "women's labor." In reality, domestic work as we know it is a fairly recent construction, dating from the last part of the nineteenth century and the first decades of the twentieth, when, under the pressure of working-class insurgency and the need for a more productive workforce, the capitalist class in England and the US began a social reform that transformed not only the factory but the community and the home and, first and foremost, the social position of women.

Seen from the point of view of its effects on women, this reform can be described as the creation of the full-time housewife, a complex process of social engineering that in a few decades removed women—especially mothers—from the factories, substantially increased male workers' wages, enough to support a "nonworking" housewife, and instituted forms of popular education to teach the female factory hands the skills required for domestic work.

This reform was not promoted only by governments and employers. Male workers too called for the exclusion of women from the factories and other waged workplaces, arguing that their place was in the home. Starting in the last decades of the nineteenth century, trade unions strongly campaigned for it, convinced that the removal of the competition of women and children would strengthen workers' bargaining power. As Wally Seccombe has shown in *Weathering the Storm: Working Class Families from the Industrial Revolution to the Fertility Decline,* by World War I, the idea of a "family wage" or "living wage" had become "a potent fixture in the labour movement and a primary objective of trade-union bargaining, endorsed by workers' parties throughout the developed capitalist world."[2] Indeed, "[b]eing able to obtain high enough wages to support one's family became a hallmark of masculine respectability, distinguishing the upper layers of the working class from the laboring poor."[3]

In this regard, the interests of the male workers and the capitalists coincided. The crisis opened by working-class struggle in England in the 1830s and 1840s, with the rise of Chartism and unionism, the beginning of a socialist movement, and the fear generated among employers by the Europe-wide workers' insurgence of 1848 "spreading like a brush fire across the continent,[4] convinced the country's rulers that improvement in the workers' lives was needed." If Britain was not to face prolonged social turmoil or even a revolution, the old strategy of compressing wages to a minimum and extending working hours to a maximum, with no time left for reproduction, had to be abandoned.

A major concern among reformers was also the growing evidence of working-class women's widespread disaffection from family and reproduction. Employed in factories all day, earning a wage of their own, used to being independent and living in a public space with other women and men for most of their waking time, English working-class women, especially factory "girls," "had no interest producing the next generation of workers";[5] they refused to take up a housework role and threatened bourgeois morality with their boisterous manners and male-like habits—like smoking and drinking.[6]

Complaints about the female workers' lack of domestic skills and wastefulness—their tendency to buy everything they needed, their inability to cook, sew, and keep a clean house, forcing their husbands to retreat to the "gin shop," their lack of maternal affection—were staples of reformers' reports from the 1840s to the turn of the century.[7] Typically, a Children Employment Commission complained in 1867 that "[b]eing employed from eight in the morning till five in the evening they [i.e., the married women] return home tired and wearied, and unwilling to make any further exertion to render the cottage comfortable," thus "when the husband returns, he finds everything uncomfortable, the cottage dirty, no meal prepared, the children tiresome and quarrelsome, the wife slatternly and cross, and his home so unpleasant to him that he not rarely betakes himself to the public house and becomes a drunkard."[8]

Even Marx remarked that "factory girls" had no domestic skills and applied their earnings to purchasing provisions once produced at home, concluding that the shutting down of the cotton mills caused by the American Civil War had at least one beneficiary effect: for the women now

> had sufficient leisure to give their infants the breast instead of poisoning them with Godfrey's Cordial [an opiate]. They also had the time to learn to cook. Unfortunately, the acquisition of this art occurred at a time when they had nothing to cook. This crisis was also utilized to teach sewing to the daughters of the workers in sewing schools. An American revolution and a universal crisis were needed in order that working girls who spin for the whole world might learn to sew![9]

Added to the concern about the crisis of domesticity that women's employment created was the fear of women's usurpation of male prerogatives, which was believed to undermine the stability of the family and trigger social unrest. During the 1847 parliamentary debates that led to the Ten Hours Act, a proponent of restricted hours for working women warned, "Female workers not only perform the labour but occupy the places of men; they are forming various clubs and associations and gradually acquiring all those privileges that are held to be the proper portion of the male sex."[10] A broken family, it was assumed, would make for an unstable country. Neglected husbands would leave the home, spend their free time in public houses, beer shops, or gin shops, and have dangerous encounters and encouraging a riotous disposition.

A further danger was that the combination of low wages, long work hours, and lack of domestic services was decimating the workforce, reducing life expectancy, and producing emaciated individuals who could not be expected to be either good workers or good soldiers.

While Marx dismissed the question of the generational reproduction of the workforce, arguing that capital could rely on the workers' "instinct for self-preservation," by the 1860s, the fear that the proletariat "was in danger of extinction" because of overwork,[11] undernourishment, and exposure to continuous epidemics was confronting the capitalist class with a major crisis. Indeed, years of overwork and underpay were severely undermining workers' capacity to reproduce themselves, the average life expectancy in the industrial areas for men being less than thirty years of age. As Wally Secombe reports:

> the vitality, health and stamina of the urban proletariat were gradually depleted in the first stage of industrialization. Laborers were washed up at an early age and their children were sick and frail. Growing up in conditions of residential squalor, people were put to work by the age of eight or ten and used up by forty, incapable of working for twelve hours a day, five and a half days a week year after year.[12]

Overworked, malnourished, living in crowded slums, industrial workers in the Lancashire mill towns had stunted lives and met early deaths. In Manchester and Liverpool, in the 1860s, they could expect to live for less than thirty years.[13] Infant mortality was also rampant and, in this case too, it was charged that maternal neglect and estrangements were the main cause. Factory inspectors, however, acknowledged that being absent from home for most of the day, female workers had no option but to leave their infants with some younger girl or an older woman who would feed them bread and water and give them abundant doses of Godfrey's Cordial, a popular opiate, to pacify them.[14] Not surprisingly factory women also tried to avoid pregnancies, often taking drugs to induce abortion.

It is against this background that we must consider the increasing outcry among the middle and upper classes, by the mid-century, against the "scandalous loss of lives" that the factory regime imposed, all the more worrisome, as conditions in other "trades" were not much better. Far from being exceptional, the living conditions in industrial towns, which reformers denounced, were duplicated in agricultural areas, where women worked as day laborers in gangs,[15] and in mine districts like North Lancashire, Cheshire, and South Wales. Here, as Marx too described it, both adult women and girls thirteen years old, or even younger, worked in the pits for eleven hours a day or more, picking up the ore, breaking the larger pieces, or, chained to go-carts, "hurrying" the coal to the horseways, half naked, at times up to their knees in water, usually with children as well.[16]

The obvious inability of the working class to reproduce itself and provide a steady flow of workers was particularly problematic, because, both in Britain and the US, the period between 1850 and the turn of the century saw a major transformation in the system of production, calling for a stronger and more productive type of worker. Generally referred to as the "Second Industrial Revolution,"[17] this was the shift from light to heavy industry. It was the change from textile production to steel, iron, and coal as the leading industrial sectors and the leading sources of capital accumulation, all made possible by the creation of an extensive rail network and the introduction of steam power.

By the 1840s, a new doctrine had begun to take hold among the architects of this new industrial revolution. It associated higher productivity and more intensive forms of labor exploitation with higher male wages, shorter hours, and, more importantly, better living conditions among the working class, to be provided by the presence in the home of laborious and thrifty wives.[18]

Decades later, in his *Principles of Economics* (1890), the English economist Alfred Marshall articulated the new industrial creed in its clearest terms. Reflecting on the conditions that guarantee the "health and strength, physical, mental and moral" of the workers, constituting, in his words, "the basis of industrial efficiency, on which the production of material wealth depends,"[19] he concluded that that a key factor was "a skilled housewife [who], with ten shillings a week to spend on food, will often do more for the health and strength of her family than an unskilled one with twenty."[20] Marshall added, "The great mortality of infants among the poor is largely due to the want of care and judgment in preparing their food; and those who do not entirely succumb to the want of motherly care often grow up with enfeebled constitutions."[21]

Marshall also stressed that the mother is "the first and by far the most powerful influence" in the determination of the *"general ability"* to work,[22] defined as:

> To be able to bear in mind many things at a time, to have everything ready when wanted, to act promptly when anything goes wrong, to accommodate oneself quickly to changes in detail of the work done, to be steady and trustworthy, to have always a reserve of force that will come out in emergency, these are the qualities which make a great industrial people. They are not peculiar to any occupation, but are wanted in all.[23]

It is no surprise, then, if, starting in the 1840s, report after report began to recommend that the number of hours that married women worked in the factories be reduced, to enable them to perform their domestic duties, and that employers abstain from hiring pregnant women. Behind the creation of the working-class housewife and the extension to the working class of the kind of home and family life once reserved to the middle class, there was the need for a new type of worker, more healthy, more robust, more productive, and, above all, more disciplined and "domesticated."

Hence the gradual expulsion of women and children from the factories, the introduction of the family wage, the schooling of women in the virtues of domesticity, in sum, a new reproductive regime and a new "social contract" that by World War I had become the norm in all industrial countries. In the US, this peaked in the decade before the beginning of the war with the rise of Fordism, in what is called the "Progressive Era."[24] According to its logic, investment in the reproduction of the working class would be matched by increased productivity, with the housewife charged with ensuring that the wage should be well spent, that the worker should be well cared for, meaning well enough to be consumed by another day of work, and the children should be well prepared for their future destiny as workers.

In England, this process began with the passage of the Mine Act of 1842, which forbade all women and boys under ten from working in the mines, and the Ten Hours Act of 1847, legislation for which workers, especially in Lancashire, had been agitating since 1833.

Other reforms were also introduced that contributed to the construction of a new working-class family and women's role as unpaid domestic laborers in the home. Wages for male workers were substantially increased, rising by 40 percent between 1862 and 1875, and more rapidly after that date, so that by 1900 they were one-third above what they had been in 1875.[25] In addition, in 1870, a national system of education was introduced, becoming compulsory in 1891. Soon after, "domestic science courses and practical lessons in domestic subjects were introduced in public elementary schools."[26]

Sanitary reforms were also introduced, including "drainage, water supply," and "street cleaning," putting a brake to recurrent epidemics.[27] A consumer market for workers began to appear, with the rise of the shop, providing for groceries but also for clothing and footwear.[28] By the 1860, associations were forming for the "protection of infant life" to convince the government to intervene against "baby farming." Schemes were proposed to punish women guilty of neglect and force the nurses they employed while at work to register and submit to inspections. There were also attempts to create day nurseries for the mothers still employed. Thus, in 1850, the first day nursery was established in Lancashire under the patronage of the mayors of Manchester and Salford. But these initiatives failed because of the resistance of female workers, who saw them as taking the bread away from older women who, no longer able to do factory work, depended for their survival on what they could earn by caring for the children of other women.[29]

Not last, the creation of the working-class family and of a healthier more productive workforce required the institution of a net separation between the housewife and the prostitute, as reformers recognized that it would not be easy to convince women to remain at home and work for free when their friends and sisters could make more money and do less work selling their bodies in the streets.

In this case too, the blame for the large number of prostitutes among the working class was placed not only on the low wages and overcrowded living conditions but on the fact that proletarian girls were not instructed about household work, which, as an article in the *Times* in 1857 argued, would have at least facilitated their export to the colonies as servants.[30] "Teach them Housewifery" was one remedy proposed to the problems posed by prostitution. At the same time, new regulations intended to increase the control of sex work and make it more degrading were introduced. First among them, were registering the lodging houses where prostitution was practiced, compulsory medical visits enforced through the Contagious Diseases Acts of 1864, 1866, and 1869, and the detention in hospitals for up to six months of those found to be diseased.[31]

Dividing the good, laborious, thrifty wife from the spendthrift prostitute was a key requirement for the constitution of the family as it emerged at the turn of the century, since dividing the "good" woman from the "bad" woman and the wife from the "whore" was a condition for the acceptance of unpaid domestic labor.

As William Acton, a doctor and social reformer, put it:

My chief interest lay in considering the effects produced upon married women by becoming accustomed to witness their vicious and profligate sisterhood flaunting it gaily, or "first rate," in their language—accepting all the attentions of men, freely plied with liquor, sitting in the best places, dressed far above their station, with plenty of money to spend, and denying themselves no amusement or enjoyment, encumbered with no domestic ties, and burdened with no children. *Whatever the purport of the drama might have been, this actual superiority of a loose life could not have escaped the attention of the quick-witted sex.*[32]

Through the separation of housewives and factory girls and, most important, housewives and prostitutes, a new sexual division of labor was produced that was distinguished by the separation of the localities in which the women worked and the social relations underlying their tasks. Respectability became the compensation for unpaid labor and dependence on men. This is the "deal" that in many ways continued until the 1960s or 1970s, when a new generation of women began to refuse it. However, opposition to the new regime developed very soon, along with the efforts of the reformers. Many proletarian women resisted the idea of being forced to work at home. As Margaret Hewitt reports, in the North of England, many women went out to work even when they did not need to, because they had developed "an extended taste for it,"[33] as they preferred "the crowded factory to the quiet home because they have a hatred of solitary housework."[34]

As the economic survival of the family came to depend on male workers, a new source of conflict developed between women and men on the use and management of the wage. Thus, payday was a day of great tension. The wives anxiously awaited their husbands' return, often trying to intercept them before they reached the pub and drank the wage away, at times sending their sons to fetch them, with physical battles often settling the matter.[35]

In the process of this great transformation, the interests of male and female workers further diverged. While the unions hailed the new domestic regime that, by World War I, had spread throughout every industrial land, women began a journey that made them more dependent on men and increasingly isolated them from each other, forcing them to work in the enclosed space of the home, with no money of their own and no limit to the hours of their work.

Accompanying these changes, the fear of a working-class revolution that had haunted the capitalist class since 1848 was largely dispelled. By the 1880s, in England, as across the Atlantic, a new predominantly male waged workforce emerged that may not have looked at the laws of the capitalist organization of work "as natural laws"—as Marx predicted it would in the course of capitalist development—but was socially and politically domesticated, clearly having new reasons for "feeling at home when not working."[36]

Notes

1   "The Construction of Domestic Work in Nineteenth-Century England and the Patriarchy of the Wage" was originally published as "Origins: The Construction of the Full-Time Housewife and Housework in 19th and 20th Century England" (Brooklyn: Idle Women, 2016).

2   Wally Seccombe, *Weathering the Storm: Working Class Families from the Industrial Revolution to the Fertility Decline* (London: Verso, 1993), 114.

3   Ibid., 114.

4   Ibid., 80.

5   Maria Mies, *Patriarchy and Accumulation on a World Scale* (London: Zed Books, 1985), 105; also see Leopoldina Fortunati, *The Arcane of Reproduction: Housework, Prostitution, Labor and Capital* (Brooklyn: Autonomedia, 1995), 171.

6   "A British factory commissioner complained: 'They often enter the beer shops, call for their pints, and smoke their pipes like men.'" According to another contemporary observer, wage-earning fostered in women "a precocious spirit of independence which weakens family ties and is highly unfavorable to the growth of domestic virtue"; Seccombe, *Weathering the Storm*, 121.

7   Margaret Hewitt, *Wives and Mothers in Victorian Industry: A Study of the Effects of the Employment of Married Women in Victorian Industry* (London: Rockliff, 1958).

8   Ibid. 70; also see Seccombe, *Weathering the Storm*, 119–20.

9   Marx, *Capital*, vol. 1, 517–18n38.

10 Judy Lown, *Women and Industrialization: Gender at Work in Nineteenth-Century England* (Minneapolis: University of Minnesota Press, 1990), 181.

11 See Fortunati, *The Arcane of Reproduction*, 170; Seccombe, *Weathering the Storm*, 77.

12 Seccombe, *Weathering the Storm*, 73.

13   Ibid., 75, 77.

14   Hewitt, *Wives and Mothers in Victorian Industry*, 152; on the use of Godfrey's Cordial see chapter 10, "Infants' Preservatives." Hewitt reports that "to soothe the distressed cries of the infants, who must have been in constant pain from their extraordinary diet, the nurses were in the habit of administering gin and peppermint and certain other nostrums, such as Godfrey's Cordial, Atkinson Royal Infants' Preservative and Mrs. Wilkinson Soothing Syrup. Thus a vicious circle was established of feeding them on bread and water and then [giving them] some more cordial, and this goes on all day. . . . The composition of these soothing syrups varied from one chemist to another, but some narcotic—opium, laudanum, morphia—was an ingredient of all"; Hewitt, ibid., 141, to which he adds: "The sales of these opiates in factory districts was enormous. In Coventry 12,000 doses of Godfrey were administered weekly, and even more proportionately in Nottingham"; ibid., 142.

15   On the "gang system" and the low standards of domestic comfort due to the employment of women in daily agricultural labor, see Ivy Pinchbeck, *Women Workers and the Industrial Revolution: 1750–1850* (New York: F.S. Crofts & Co., 1930), 86–87, 106–7.

16   Ibid., chapter 11, 240ff, especially 244–45, 247–48, 249.

17   On the "Second Industrial Revolution," see Seccombe, *Weathering the Storm*, chapter 4; Eric Hobsbawm, *Industry and Empire: The Making of Modern English Society, 1759 to the Present Day* (New York: Pantheon Books, 1968), chapter 6.

18   E.J. Hobsbawm, *Industry and Empire*, 101 ff.

19   Alfred Marshall, *Principles of Economics: An Introductory Volume* (London: Macmillan and Co., 1938), 193.

20   Ibid., 195.

21   Ibid., 195–96.

22   As Marshall put it: "General ability depends largely on the surrounding of childhood and youth. In this the first and by far the most powerful influence is that of the mother"; ibid., 207. For this reason, Marshall opposed women working for wages. He noted that infant mortality "is generally higher, especially where there are many mothers who neglect their familial duties in order to earn money wages"; ibid., 198.

23   Ibid., 206–7.

24   On this subject, among others, see Mariarosa Dalla Costa, *Family Welfare and the State between Progressivism and the New Deal* (New York: Common Notions, 2015 [1997]); Nancy Folbre, "The Unproductive Housewife: Her Evolution in Nineteenth-Century Economic Thought," *Signs* 16, no. 3 (Spring 1991): 463–84.

25   Hobsbawm, *Industry and Empire*, 133. "[B]y the early 1870s trade unionism was officially recognized and accepted"; ibid., 128.

26   Ibid., 79.

27   Ibid., 131.

28   Ibid., 136.

29   Ibid., 166.

30   William Acton, *Prostitution*, edited and with an introduction by Peter
     Fryer (New York: Frederick A. Praeger Publishers, 1969 [1857]), 210–11.
31   Ibid., 232n1.
32   Ibid., 54–55.
33   Hewitt, *Wives and Mothers in Victorian Industry*, 191.
34   Ibid.
35   Seccombe, *Weathering the Storm*, 146–54.
36   The reference here is to Marx's discussion of "estranged labor," i.e., the
     fact that since work in capitalism is for the worker an alienating activ-
     ity, "[t]he worker therefore only feels himself outside his work, and in
     his work he feel outside himself, and when he is working he is not at
     home. He is at home when he is not working. His labour is therefore
     not voluntary but forced labour"; Karl Marx, *Economic and Philosophical
     Manuscripts of 1844*, trans. Martin Milligan (Moscow: Foreign Languages
     Publishing House 1961), 72.

SEVEN

Origins and Development of Sexual Work in the United States and Britain[1]

From the beginning of capitalist society, sexual work has performed two fundamental functions in the context of capitalist production and the capitalist division of labor. On the one hand, it has ensured the procreation of new workers. On the other hand, it has been a key aspect of their daily reproduction, as sexual release has been, for men at least, the safety valve for the tensions accumulated during the workday, all the more indispensable, as for a long time sex was one of the few pleasures conceded to them. The very concept of the "proletariat" signified a working class that reproduced itself prolifically, not only because one more child meant another factory hand and another pay but also because sex was the only pleasure available to the poor.

Despite its importance, during the first phase of industrialization, the sexual activity of the working class was not subjected to much state regulation. In this phase, which lasted until the second half of the nineteenth century, the main concern of the capitalist class was the quantity rather than the quality of the labor power to be produced. That the English workers, male and female, died on average at about thirty-five years of age did not matter to the British factory owners, as long as those years were spent in a factory, from sunup to sundown, from the first years of life until death, and as long as new labor power was abundantly procreated to replace those continually eliminated.[2] English workers, male and female, were expected to produce an abundant proletariat, and little consideration was given to their "moral conduct." Indeed, it was expected that promiscuousness would be a norm in the slum dormitories where, in Glasgow as in New York, workers spent the few hours they had away from the factory. It was also expected that English and American female workers would alternate or integrate factory work with prostitution, which exploded in these countries in conjunction with the takeoff of the industrialization process.[3]

It was in the second half of the nineteenth century that things started to change, as, under the pressure of working-class struggle, a restructuring of production took place that demanded a different type of worker and, accordingly, a change in the process of its reproduction. It was the shift from light industry to heavy industry, from the mechanical frame to the steam engine, from the production of cloth to that of coal and steel, that created the need for a worker less emaciated, less prone to disease, and more capable of sustaining the intense rhythms of work that the shift to heavy industry required. It was in this context that the capitalist class, generally indifferent to the high mortality rates of the industrial workers, crafted a new reproduction strategy, increasing the male wage, and returning proletarian women to the home, while at the same time increasing the intensity of factory work, which the better reproduced waged worker would now be capable of performing.

Thus, hand in hand with the introduction of Taylorism and a new regimentation of the work process, in the second half of the nineteenth century we have a reform of the working-class family centered on the construction of a new domestic role for the woman that would make her the guarantor of the production of a more qualified workforce. This meant enticing women not only to procreate to fill the ranks of the workforce but to guarantee the daily reproduction of the laborers through the provision of the physical, emotional, and sexual services necessary to reintegrate their capacity to work.

As mentioned, the reorganization of work that took place in England between 1850 and 1880 was dictated by the need to secure a healthier, more disciplined, and more productive labor force and, above all, to break the surge of working-class organization. A further consideration, however, was the realization that the recruitment of women into the factories had destroyed their acceptance of and capacity for reproductive work to such an extent that if remedies were not found, the reproduction of the English working class would be severely jeopardized. It suffices to read the reports periodically drafted by government-appointed factory inspectors in England between 1840 and 1880 on the conduct of the female factory hands to realize that more was at stake in the advocated change of reproductive regime than concern for the health and combativeness of the male part of the working class.

Undisciplined, indifferent to housework, family, and morality, determined to have a good time in the few hours free from work available to them, ready to leave the home for the street or the bar, where they would drink and smoke like men, alienated from their children, married or unmarried, female factory hands, in the bourgeois imagination, were a threat to the production of a stable labor force and had to be domesticated. It was in this context that the "domestication" of the working-class family and the creation of the full-time working-class housewife became a state policy, also inaugurating a new form of capital accumulation.

As if suddenly awakened to the reality of factory life, by the 1850s, a host of reformers began to thunder against the long hours women spent away from the home, and by means of "protective legislation" first eliminated female night shifts and later ousted married women from the factories, so that they could be reeducated to function like the "angels of the hearth," cognizant of the arts of patience and subordination, especially since the work to which they were destined was not to be paid.

The idealization of "female virtue," until the turn of the century reserved for the women of the middle and upper class, was thus extended to working-class women to hide the unpaid labor expected of them. Not surprisingly, we see in this period a new ideological campaign promoting among the working class the ideals of *maternity* and *love*, understood as the capacity for absolute self-sacrifice. Fantine, the prostitute mother of *Les Misérables*, who sells her hair and two of her teeth to support her infant child, was a proper embodiment of this ideal. "Conjugal love" and "motherly instinct" are themes that permeate the discourse of Victorian reformers, together with complaints about the pernicious effects of factory work on women's morality and reproductive role.

Regulating housework would not be possible, however, without regulating sexual work. As with housework, what characterized the sexual politics of capital and the state in this phase was the extension to the proletarian woman of the principles already regulating the sexual conduct of women in the bourgeois family. First among them was the negation of female sexuality as a source of pleasure and monetary gain for women. For the transformation of the female factory worker-prostitute—in both cases a paid worker—into an unpaid mother-wife ready to sacrifice her own interests and desires for the well-being of her family, an essential premise was the "purification" of the maternal role of any erotic element.

This meant that the wife-mother should only enjoy the pleasure of "love," conceived of as a sentiment free from any desire for sex or remuneration. In sexual work itself, the division of labor between "sex for procreation" and "sex for pleasure," and, in the case of women, the association of sex with antisocial characteristics, was deepened. Both in the US and England, a new regulation of prostitution was introduced that aimed to separate "honest women" from "prostitutes"—a distinction which the recruitment of women into factory work had dissipated. William Acton, one of the promoters of the reform in England, noted how pernicious was the constant presence of prostitutes in public places. The reasons he offered speak volumes:

> My chief interest lay in considering the effect produced upon married women by becoming accustomed at these *réunions* to witness the vicious and profligate sisterhood flaunting it gaily, or "first rate" in their language, accepting all the attentions of men, freely plied with liquor, sitting in the best places, dressed far above their station, with plenty of money to spend, denying themselves no

amusements or enjoyment, encumbered with no domestic duties, and burdened with no children. Whatever the purport of the drama might have been, this actual superiority of a loose life could not have escaped the attention of the quick-witted sex.[4]

Acton's initiative was also prompted by another concern: the spread of venereal diseases, syphilis in particular, among the proletariat:

> The reader who is a conscientious parent must perforce support me; for, were the sanitary measures I advocate in operation, with what diminished anxiety would he not contemplate the progress of his boys from infancy to manhood? The statesman and the political economists are mine already, for are not armies and navies invalidated—is not labour enfeebled—is not even population deteriorated by the evils against which I propose we should contend?[5]

Regulating prostitution meant subjecting sex workers to medical control, in line with the model adopted in France in the first half of the nineteenth century.

Along with this regulation, which made the state, through the police and the medical profession, the direct supervisor of sex work, we have *the institutionalization of the prostitute and the mother as separate, mutually exclusive female figures and functions, that is, the institutionalization of maternity without pleasure and "pleasure" without maternity*. Social policy began to require that the prostitute not become a mother.[6] Her maternity had to be hidden, removed from the place of work. In the literature of the time, the child of the prostitute lives in the countryside, consigned to charitable caretakers. By contrast, the mother, the spouse, the "honest woman," would be expected to look at sex only as a domestic service, a conjugal duty that she could not escape, but which would give her no pleasure. The only sex conceded to the mother would be the sex made clean by marriage and procreation—that is, by endless hours of unpaid labor, consumed with little joy, and always accompanied by the fear of impregnation. Hence, the classic image, handed down to us from nineteenth-century novels, of the woman suffering the advances of her husband, careful not to contradict the aura of sanctity by which society wanted to encircle her head.

The division of the labors of sex work and mothering, however, has been possible only because capital has used much psychological and physical violence to impose it. The destiny of the unwed mother, the "seduced and abandoned" that, together with the exaltation of motherly sacrifices, filled the pages of nineteenth-century literature, has been a constant warning to women that anything was preferable to "losing one's honor" and being considered a "slut." But the whip that has most served to keep women in place has been the condition in which the prostitute, at the proletarian level, has been forced to live, as she was increasingly isolated from other women and subjected to constant state control.

But despite the criminalization of prostitution, efforts to create a respectable working-class family were long frustrated. Only a small part of the male working class benefitted from the kind of wages that would enable a family to survive on "his job" alone, and sex work was always the most readily available form of income for proletarian women, one to which they were forced by the volatility of sexual affairs that often left them alone with children to support. It was a sobering discovery to learn in Italy, in the 1970s, that before World War I most proletarian children had been registered at birth as fathered by "NN" (*nomen nescio*; name unknown). Employers took advantage of the poverty of women to force them into prostitution to keep whatever jobs they might have or to prevent their husbands from being laid off.

As for the "honest" working-class women, they have always known that the dividing line between marriage and prostitution, between the whore and the respectable woman, is very thin. Proletarian women have always known that for women marriage meant being "a servant by day and a whore at night";[7] if they planned to abandon the conjugal bed, they had to reckon with poverty. Still, the construction of female sexuality as a service, and its negation as pleasure, have long kept alive the idea that female sexuality is sinful and redeemable only through marriage and procreation and produced a situation where *every woman is considered a potential prostitute* to be constantly controlled. As a result, before the rise of the feminist movement, generations of women have lived their sexuality as something shameful and have had to prove that they were not prostitutes. At the same time, prostitution, though an object of social condemnation to be controlled by the state, has been recognized as a necessary component of the reproduction of labor power, precisely because it has been assumed that the wife would not be able to completely satisfy her husband's sexual needs.

This explains why *sexual work was the first aspect of housework that was socialized*. The state brothel, the *casa chiusa* (closed house) or *maison des femmes*, typical of the first phase of capital's planned sexual work, *has institutionalized the woman as a collective lover, working directly or indirectly at the service of the state as the collective husband and pimp*. Besides ghettoizing women who would be paid to perform what millions provided for free, the socialization of sexual work responded to criteria for productive efficiency. The *Taylorization of coitus* typical of the brothel has greatly increased the productivity of sexual work. Low-cost, easily accessible, state-sponsored sex was ideal for a worker who, after spending a day in a factory or an office, would not have the time and energy to look for amorous adventures or embark on the path of voluntary relations.

The Struggle against Sexual Work

With the rise of the nuclear family and marital sex a new phase in the history of women's struggle against housework and sexual work began. Evidence of this struggle is the increase in divorce at the turn of the twentieth century, above all in the US and England, and among the middle class, where the nuclear family model was first adopted.

As William O'Neill points out, "Until about the middle of the nineteenth century divorces were a rare events in the

Western world; thereafter they occurred at such a steadily increasing rate that by the end of the century the legal dissolution of marriage was recognized as a major social phenomenon."[8] He continues: "If we consider the Victorian family as a new institution . . . we can see why divorce became a necessary part of the family system. When the family becomes the center of social organization, its intimacy becomes suffocating, its constraints unbearable and its expectations too high to be realized."[9]

O'Neill and his contemporaries were well aware that behind the family crisis and the rush to divorce there was the rebellion of women. In the US, the bulk of the requests for divorce were presented by women. Divorce was not the only way in which women expressed their refusal of family discipline. In this same period, both in the US and England, the fertility rate began to fall. From 1850 to 1900, the average family in the US shrank by one member. Simultaneously, in both countries, inspired by the slave abolitionist movement, a feminist movement developed that targeted "domestic slavery."

"Are Women to Blame?"—the title of a symposium on divorce—published by the *North American Review* in 1889, was a typical example of the attack launched against women in this period. Women were accused of being greedy or selfish, of expecting too much from marriage, of having a weak sense of responsibility, and of subordinating the common well-being to their narrow personal interest. Even when they did not divorce, women carried on a daily struggle against housework and sexual work, often taking the form of illness and desexualization. As early as 1854, Mary Nichols, an American doctor and promoter of family reform, would write:

> Nine tenths of the children born are not desired by the mother. . . . A vast number of the women of civilization have neither the sexual nor maternal passion. All women want love and support. They do not want to bear children or to be harlots for this love or this support. In marriage as it at present exists the instinct against bearing children and against submitting to amative embrace,

is almost as general as the love for children after they are born. The obliteration of the maternal and sexual instinct in woman is a terrible pathological fact.[10]

Women used the excuse of feebleness, fragility, and sudden illnesses (migraines, fainting, hysteria) to avoid conjugal duties and the danger of unwanted pregnancies. That these were not, properly speaking, "illnesses" but forms of resistance to housework and sexual work is demonstrated not only by the pervasive character of this phenomena but also by the complaints of the husbands and the sermons of the doctors. This is how an American doctor, Mrs. R.B. Gleason, described the dialectics of illness and refusal, viewed both from a woman's and a man's point of view in the turn of the century middle-class family.

Says the wife:
I ought never to have been married, for my life is one prolonged agony. I could endure it myself alone, but the thought that I am, from year to year, becoming the mother of those who are to partake of and perpetuate the misery that I endure, makes me so wretched that I am well-nigh distracted.

Says the doctor:
The prospective husband may take great care to protect the fair but frail one of his choice; he may . . . fondly cherish the wife of his youth when she aches constantly and ages prematurely; still he has no helpmate—no one to double life's joys or lighten life's labors for him. Some sick women grow selfish and forget that, in a partnership such as theirs, others suffer when they suffer. Every true husband has but half a life who has a sick wife.

Says the husband:
Can she ever be well?[11]

When they did not fall ill, women became frigid or, in Mary Nichols's words, they inherited "an apathetic state that does not impel them to any material union."[12] In the context of a sexual discipline that denied women, especially in the middle class, control over their sexual lives, frigidity and the proliferation of bodily aches were effective forms of refusal that could be masked as an extension of the normal defense of chastity, that is, as an excess of virtue that allowed women to turn the tables to their advantage and present themselves as the true defenders of sexual morality. In this way, middle-class Victorian women were often able to refuse their sexual duties more than their grand-daughters would be able to. After decades of women's refusal of sexual work, psychologists, sociologists, and other "experts" have wised up and are now less ready to retreat. Today, in fact, a whole campaign is mounted that guilt-trips the "frigid woman," not least with the charge of not being liberated.

The blossoming of the social sciences in the nineteenth century must in part be connected to the crisis of the family and women's refusal of it. Psychoanalysis was born as the science of sexual control, charged with providing strategies for the reform of family relations. In both the US and England, plans for the reformation of sexuality emerged in the first decade of the twentieth century. Books, booklets, pamphlets, essays, and treatises were devoted to the family and the "divorce problem," revealing not only the depth of the crisis but also the growing awareness that a new sexual/family ethics would be needed. Thus, while in the US the more conservative circles founded the League for the Protection of the Family, and radical women advocated free unions and argued that for this system to work "it would be necessary for the state to subsidize all mothers as a matter of right,"[13] sociologists and psychologists joined the debate, proposing that the problem be scientifically resolved. It would be Freud's task to systematize the new sexual code, which is why his work became so popular in both countries.

Freud and the Reform of Sexual Work
On the surface, Freud's theory seems to concern sexuality in general, but its real target was female sexuality. Freud's work was a response to women's refusals of housework, procreation, and sexual work. As his writings well indicate, he was deeply aware

that the "family crisis" stemmed from the fact that women did not want to or could not do their job. He was also concerned for the growth of male impotence, which had assumed such proportions as to be described by him as one of the main social phenomena of his time. Freud attributed the latter to the "extension of the demands made upon women onto the sexual life of the male, and the taboo on sexual intercourse except in monogamous marriage." He wrote: "Civilized sexual morality . . . by glorifying monogamy . . . cripples virile selection—the sole influence by which an improvement of the race can be obtained."[14]

The struggle of women against sexual work not only jeopardized their role as domestic lovers and produced disaffected males, it also put at risk their role as procreators (perhaps more important at the time). Freud wrote:

> I do not know if the anaesthetic type of women is also found outside of civilized education, but I consider it probable. In any case, these women who conceive without pleasure show later little willingness to endure frequent childbirths, accompanied as they are by pain, so that the training that precedes marriage directly frustrates the very aim of marriage.[15]

Freud's strategy was to (re)integrate sex into the domestic workday and discipline in order to reconstruct the woman's traditional role of wife and mother on more solid bases, by means of a freer and satisfying sexual life. In other words, with Freud, *sexuality is placed at the service of the consolidation of housework* and is turned into an element of work, soon to become itself a duty. Freud's prescription is a freer sexuality for a healthier family life and for a family in which the woman would identify with her wifely function instead of becoming hysterical, neurotic, and enveloping herself in frigidity after the first months of marriage and perhaps being tempted to transgress through "degenerate" experiences such as lesbianism.

Beginning with Freud, sexual liberation for women has meant an intensification of domestic work. The model of the wife and mother cultivated by the psychology profession was no longer that of the mother-procreator of abundant offspring but that of the wife-lover who had to guarantee higher levels of pleasure to her husband than what was obtainable from the simple penetration of a passive or resistant body.

In the United States, the reintegration of sexuality into housework began to take hold in the proletarian family with the development of domesticity in the Progressive Era and accelerated with the Fordist reorganization of work and wages. It came with the assembly line, the five-dollar-a-day wage, and the work speed-up, which demanded that the men rest at night instead of prowling around in the saloons, so as to be fresh and restored for another day of hard work. The strict work discipline and speed-up that Taylorism and Fordism introduced into the American factory required a new hygiene, a new sexual regime, and, therefore, the reconversion of sexuality and family life. In other words, for the workers to be able to sustain the regimentation of factory life, the wage had to buy a more substantial sexuality than that provided by the casual encounters in the saloons. Making the home more attractive through the reorganization of home-based sexual work was also vital at a time of rising wages, which might otherwise be spent on merrymaking.

The shift was also prompted by political considerations. The attempt to win men over to the home and away from the saloon, which intensified after World War I, was prompted by the saloon having been a center for political organizing and debate, as well as for prostitution.

For the housewife this reorganization meant that she would have to continue to make children, but she would have to worry that her hips might become too large (this is how the Calvary of diets began). She would continue washing dishes and floors but with polished nails and frills on her apron, and she would continue to slave from sunup to sundown but would have to spruce herself up to adequately greet her husband's return. At this point, saying no in bed became more difficult. In fact, new canons publicized by psychology books and women's magazines began to stress that the sexual union was crucial for a well-functioning marriage.

Starting in the in the 1950s, there was also a change in the function of prostitution. As the century progressed, the average American male resorted to prostitution for the satisfaction of his needs less and less. What saved the family, however, more than anything else, was the limited access that women had to wages of their own. Nonetheless, all was not well within the American family, as seen in the high number of divorces in the postwar period (both in England and the United States). The more that was asked of women and the family, the more women's refusal grew, which could not yet be a refusal of marriage for obvious economic reasons but was, rather, *a demand for higher mobility within marriage*—that is, a demand to be able to move from husband to husband (as from employer to employer), exacting better conditions of housework. In this period, the struggle for the second job (and for welfare) became closely connected with the struggle against the family, as, for women, the factory or the office often represented the only alternative to unpaid house-work, to their isolation within the family, and to subordination to their husbands' desires. Not accidentally, for a long time, men saw women's second job as the antechamber to prostitution. Until the upsurge in the welfare struggle, having an outside job was often the only way for women to get out of the house, to meet people, and to escape an insufferable marriage.

Already at the beginning of the 1950s, the Kinsey Report rang an alarm bell, as it demonstrated women's resistance to expending adequate levels of sexual work. It was discovered that many American women were frigid, that they did not participate in their sex work but only went through the motions. It was also discovered that half of American males had or wanted to have homosexual relations. Similar conclusions were reached by an investigation on marriage in the American working class conducted a few years later. Here too it was found that a quarter of married women made love only as a pure conjugal duty, and an extremely high number of them did not derive any pleasure from it.[16] It was at this point that capital in the US launched a massive campaign on the sexual front, determined to defeat with the arms of theory and practice the obstinate apathy of so many women toward sexuality. The dominant theme in this campaign was the quest for the female orgasm, increasingly taken as the test of perfection in the conjugal union. In the 1960s, the female orgasm became the motif of a whole series of psychological studies, culminating with Masters and Johnson's alleged epochal discovery that not only did female orgasm exist, but it existed in multiple forms.

With the Masters and Johnson experiments, the productivity required of women's sexual work was fixed at very high quotas. Not only could women make love and reach orgasm, *they had to*. If we did not succeed, we were not real women— even worse, we were not "liberated." This message was communicated to us in the 1960s from movie screens, the pages of women's magazines, and the "do-it-yourself" handbooks that taught us the positions enabling us to copulate satisfactorily. It was also preached by psychoanalysts who established that "full" sexual relations are a condition for social and psychological balance. By the 1970s, "sex clinics" and "sex shops" began to appear, and family life underwent a remarkable restructuring, with the legitimization of premarital and extramarital relations, "open marriage," and group sex and the acceptance of auto-eroticism. Meanwhile, just to be safe, technological innovation produced the vibrator for those women who even the latest updating of the Kama Sutra could not put to work.

What Has This Meant for Women?
Let us state it in no uncertain terms. For the women of today no less than for our mothers and grandmothers, sexual liberation can only mean liberation from "sex," rather than the intensification of sexual work.

"Liberation from sex" means liberation from the conditions in which we are forced to live our sexuality, which transform this activity into arduous work, full of incognita and accidents, not least the danger of repeatedly getting pregnant, given that even the latest contraceptives are taken at a considerable health risk. Until these conditions prevail, any "progress" brings more work and anxiety. Undoubtedly, it is a great advantage not to be lynched by fathers, brothers, and husbands if it is discovered that we are not virgins or that we are "unfaithful" and "misbehave"—although, the number of women murdered by their partners because they wish to leave them is constantly growing. For us, sexuality continues to be a source of anxiety, as "sexual liberation" has been turned into a duty that we must accept if we do not want to be accused of being backward. Thus, while our grandmothers could go to sleep in peace after a day of hard work with the excuse of a migraine, we, their liberated granddaughters, feel guilty when we refuse to have sex, do not actively participate in it, or even fail to enjoy it.

To come, to have an orgasm, has become such a categorical imperative that we feel uneasy admitting that "nothing is happening," and to men's insistent questions we respond with a lie or force ourselves to make another effort, with the result that often our beds feel like a gym.

But the main difference is that our mothers and grandmothers looked at sexual services within a logic of exchange: you went to bed with the man you married, that is, the man who promised you a certain financial security. Today, instead, we work for free, in bed and the kitchen, not only because sexual work is unpaid but because increasingly we provide sexual services without expecting anything in return. Indeed, the symbol of the liberated woman is the woman who is always available but in return no longer asks for anything.

Notes

1   "Origins and Development of Sexual Work in the United States and Britain" was originally published in Silvia Federici, *Beyond the Periphery of the Skin: Rethinking, Remaking, Reclaiming the Body in Contemporary Capitalism* (Oakland: PM Press, 2020).

2   It is significant, for instance, that in the US, throughout the nineteenth century, the age of consent for females was set at about ten.

3   It is generally recognized that low female wages and the promiscuous mixing of the sexes in the slums were the main causes of the "explosion" of prostitution that took place in England in the first phase of the industrialization process. As William Acton wrote in his famous work on prostitution: "Many women . . . swell the ranks of prostitution through being by their position particularly exposed to temptation. The women to whom this remark applies are chiefly actresses, milliners, shop-girls,

domestic servants and women employed in factories or working in agricultural gangs. . . . It is a shameful fact, but nonetheless true, that the lowness of the wage paid to the work-women in various trades is a fruitful source of prostitution"; William Acton, *Prostitution*, edited and with an introduction by Peter Fryer (New York: Frederick A. Praeger Publishers, 1969 [1857]), 129–30. Not surprisingly, for a long time, in the bourgeois family, the promiscuous or "immoral" conduct of women was punished as a form of *déclassement*. "To behave like one of those women" meant to behave like proletarian women, the women of the "lower classes."

4   Ibid., 54–55.

5   Ibid., 27.

6   This, however, was not an easy task. Significantly, Acton lamented: "Prostitutes do not, as is generally supposed, die in harness . . . on the contrary, they, for the most part, become, sooner or later, with tarnished bodies and polluted minds, wives and mothers, while among some classes of the people the moral sentiment is so depraved that the woman who lives by the hire of her person is received on almost equal terms to social intercourse. It is clear, then, that though we may call these women outcasts and pariahs, they have a powerful influence for evil on all ranks of the community. The moral injury inflicted on society by prostitution is incalculable; the physical injury is at least as great"; ibid., 84–85.

7   This is how the grandmother of a feminist friend described her life.

8   7. William O'Neill, *Divorce in the Progressive Era* (New Haven, CT: Yale University Press, 1967), 1.

9   Ibid., 86

10 Quoted in Nancy F. Cott, ed., *Roots of Bitterness: Documents of the Social History of American Women* (New York: E.P. Dutton, 1972), 286.

11 Ibid., 274.

12 Ibid., 286.

13 O'Neil, *Divorce in the Progressive Era*, 104.

14 Sigmund Freud, "Civilized Sexual Morality and Modern Nervousness" (1908), in Sigmund Freud, *Sexuality and the Psychology of Love* (New York: Colliers Books, 1972), 11.

15 Ibid., 25.

16 Mirra Komarovsky, *Blue-Collar Marriage* (New York: Vintage Books, 1967), 83.

Bibliography

Acton, William. *Prostitution*. Edited with an introduction by Peter Fryer. New York: Frederick A. Praeger Publishers, 1969 [1857].

Anderson, Kevin B. "Marx's Late Writings on Non-Western and Societies and Gender." *Rethinking Marxism* 14, no. 4 (Winter 2002): 84–96.

Bebel, August. *Woman under Socialism*. New York: Schocken Books, 1971 [1883].

Bellamy Foster, John. "Marx and the Environment." *Monthly Review* 47, no. 3 (July–August 1995): 108–23.

———. "Marx and the Rift in the Universal Metabolism of Nature." *Monthly Review* 65, no. 7 (December 2013): 1–19.

———. "Women, Nature and Capital in the Industrial Revolution." *Monthly Review* 69, no. 8 (January 2018): 1–25.

Bellamy Foster, John, and Brett Clark. *The Robbery of Nature: Capitalism and the Ecological Rift*. New York: Monthly Review Press, 2020.

Blackstone, William. *Commentaries on the Law of England*. Oxford: Clarendon Press, 1765–1770.

Bock, Gisela, and Barbara Duden. "Labor of Love—Love as Labor: On the Genesis of Housework in Capitalism." In Edith Hoshino Altback, ed. *From Feminism to Liberation*. Rev. ed. Cambridge, MA: Schenkman Publishing Company, 1980, 153–92.

Bonefeld, Werner, Richard Gunn, John Holloway, and Kosmas Psychopedis. "Introduction: Emancipating Marx." In Bonefeld, Gunn, Holloway, and Psychopedis, *Emancipating Marx*, 1–6.

Bonefeld, Werner, Richard Gunn, John Holloway, and Kosmas Psychopedis, eds. *Emancipating Marx: Open Marxism* 3. London: Pluto Press 1995.

Boutang, Yann Moulier. *De l'esclavage au salariat: Économie historique du salariat bride*. Paris: Presses Universitaires de France, 1998.

Bridenthal, Renate, Claudia Koonz, and Susan Stuard, eds. *Becoming Visible: Women in European History*. 2nd ed. Boston: Houghton Mifflin Co., 1987.

Brown, Heather A. *Marx on Gender and the Family: A Critical Study*. Historical Materialism 39. London: Brill, 2012.

Caffentzis, George. "A Critique of 'Cognitive Capitalism.'" In George Caffentzis. *In Letters of Blood and Fire: Work, Machines, and the Crisis of Capitalism*. Oakland: PM Press, 2013, 95–123.

————. "From the Grundrisse to Capital and Beyond: Then and Now." *Workplace: A Journal for Academic Labor* no. 15 (September 2008): 59–74.

Chevalier, Louis. *Classes laborieuses et classes dangereuses à Paris au XIX siècle.* Paris: Plon, 1958.

Cleaver, Harry. Introduction to Antonio Negri, *Marx beyond Marx,* xix–xxvii.

————. *Reading Capital Politically.* Leeds: Anti/Theses, 2000.

Cockburn, Cynthia. "The Standpoint Theory." In Mojab, *Marxism and Feminism,* 331–46.

Conner, Clifford. D. *A People's History of Science: Miners, Midwives, and Low Mechanicks.* New York: Nation Books, 2005.

Custer, Peter. *Capital Accumulation and Women's Labor in Asian Economies.* New York: Monthly Review Press, 2012 [1995].

Dalla Costa, Mariarosa. "Capitalism and Reproduction." In Bonefeld, Gunn, Holloway, and Psychopedis. *Emancipating Marx.* 1995, 7–16.

————. "Community, Factory and School from the Woman's Viewpoint." *L'Offensiva, Quaderni di Lotta Femminista* no. 1. Torino: Musolini Editore, 1972.

————. *Family Welfare and the State Between Progressivism and the New Deal.* New York: Common Notions, 2015 [1997].

————. "Reproduction and Emigration" (1974). In Dalla Costa, *Women and the Subversion of the Community,* 69–108.

————. "Women and the Subversion of the Community" (1975). In *Women and the Subversion of the Community,* 18–49.

————. *Women and the Subversion of the Community: A Mariarosa Dalla Costa Reader.* Oakland: PM Press, 2019.

De Angelis, Massimo. *The Beginning of History: Value Struggles and Global Capital.* London: Pluto Press, 2007.

Draper, Hal. *The Adventures of the Communist Manifesto.* Berkeley: Center for Socialist History, 1998.

Du Bois, W.E.B. "Marxism and the Negro Problem." *Crisis* (May 1933).

Eckerseley, Robyn. "Socialism and Eco-centrism: Towards a New Synthesis." In Ted Benton, ed. *The Greening of Marxism.* New York: Guildford Press, 1996, 272–97.

The Ecologist. *Whose Common Future? Reclaiming the Commons.* Philadelphia: Earthscan, 1993.

Engels, Frederick. *The Condition of the Working Class in England.* Moscow: Progress Publishers, 1980 [1845].

————. *The Housing Question.* Moscow: Progress Publishers, 1979 [1872].

Fanon, Frantz. *The Wretched of the Earth.* New York: Grove, 1986 [1961].

Fauré, Christine. *Political and Historical Encyclopedia of Women.* New York: Routledge, 2003.

Federici, Silvia. *Beyond the Periphery of the Skin: Rethinking, Remaking, and Reclaiming the Body in Contemporary Capitalism.* Oakland: PM Press, 2019.

————. *Caliban and the Witch: Women, the Body and Primitive Accumulation.* Brooklyn: Autonomedia, 2004.

————. "Capital and Gender." In Ingo Schmidt and Carlo Fanelli, eds. *Reading Capital Today.* London: Pluto Press, 2017, 79–96.

———. *El Patriarcado del salario. Crítica feminista al marxismo.* Madrid: Traficantes de Sueños, 2018.

———. "Feminism and the Politics of the Commons in an Era of Primitive Accumulation." In *Revolution at Point Zero*, 138–48.

———. "Origins and Development of Sexual Work in the United States and Britain" (1978). In *Beyond the Periphery of the Skin*, 2020, 89–106.

———. *Re-enchanting the World: Feminism and the Politics of the Commons.* Oakland: PM Press, 2019.

———. *Revolution at Point Zero: Housework, Reproduction, and Feminist Struggle.* Rev. ed. Oakland: PM Press, 2020.

———. "War, Globalization and Reproduction." In *Revolution at Point Zero*, 76–84.

———. "Witch-Hunting, Globalization, and Feminist Solidarity in Africa Today." *Journal of International Women's Studies* 10, no. 1 (October 2008): 21–35.

———. "Women, Land Struggle and the Reconstruction of the Commons!' *Working USA* 14, no. 1 (March 2011): 41–56.

Federici, Silvia, and Arlen Austin eds. *The New York Wages for Housework Committee: History, Theory, Documents, 1972–1977.* Brooklyn: Autonomedia, 2019.

Ferber, Marianne A., and Julie N. Nelson, eds. *Beyond Economic Man: Feminist Theory and Economics.* Chicago: University of Chicago Press, 1993.

Ferrari Bravo, Luciano. "Vecchie e nuove questioni nella teoria dell'imperialismo." Introduction to Luciano Ferrari Bravo, ed. *Imperialismo e classe operaia multinazionale.* Milano: Feltrinelli, 1975, 7–67.

Folbre, Nancy. "Nursebots to the Rescue? Immigration, Automation, and Care," *Globalizations* 3, no. 3 (September 2006): 349–60.

———. "Socialism, Feminist and Scientific." In Marianne A. Ferber and Julie A. Nelson, eds. *Beyond Economic Man.*

———. "The Unproductive Housewife: Her Evolution in Nineteenth-Century Economic Thought." *Signs* 16, no. 3 (Spring 1991): 463–84.

Fortunati, Leopoldina. *The Arcane of Reproduction: Housework, Prostitution, Labor and Capital.* Brooklyn: Autonomedia, 1995 [1981].

Foster, John. *Class Struggle and the Industrial Revolution: Early Industrial Capitalism in Three English Towns.* London: Methuen & Co., 1974.

Fourier, Charles. *Design for Utopia: Selected Writings of Charles Fourier.* New York: Schocken Books, 1971.

———. *The Utopian Vision of Charles Fourier: Selected Texts on Work, Love, and Passionate Attraction.* Edited and translated by Jonathan Beecher and Richard Bienvenu. Boston: Beacon, 1971.

Frank, Andre Gunder. *Capitalism and Underdevelopment in Latin America.* New York: Monthly Review Press, 1969 [1967].

Frisken, Amanda. *Victoria Woodhull's Sexual Revolution: Political Theater and Popular Press in Nineteenth-Century America.* Philadelphia: University of Pennsylvania Press, 2004.

Giménez, Martha E. "Capitalism and the Oppression of Women: Marx Revisited." *Science and Society* 69, no. 1 (January 2005):11–32.

————. *Marx, Women, and Capitalist Social Reproduction: Marxist Feminist Essays*. Chicago: Haymarket Books, 2018.

Gorz, André. *A Farewell to the Working Class*. London: Pluto Press, 1982.

————. *Paths to Paradise: On the Liberation from Work*. London: Pluto Press, 1985.

Graeber, David. *Fragments of an Anarchist Anthropology*. Chicago: Prickly Paradigm Press, 1993.

Gramsci, Antonio. "Americanism and Fordism." In *Selections from the Prison Notebooks*. London: Lawrence & Wishart, 1971, 277–318.

Granter, Edward. *Critical Social Theory and the End of Work*. Burlington, VT: Ashgate, 2009.

Guitierrez Aguilar, Raquel. *Los Ritmos del Pachakuti. Levantamiento y Movilizacion En Bolivia (2000–2005)*. Miguel Hidalgo, MX: Sisifo Ediciones, 2009.

Harding, Sandra, and Merrill B. Hintikka, eds. *Discovering Reality: Feminist Perspectives on Epistemology, Metaphysics, Methodology, and Philosophy of Science*. Dordrecht, NL: D. Reidel Publishing Company, 1983.

Hardt, Michael, and Antonio Negri. *Commonwealth*. Cambridge, MA: Harvard University Press, 2009.

————. *Empire*. Cambridge, MA: Harvard University Press, 2000.

————. *Multitude: War and Democracy in the Age of Empire*. Minneapolis: University of Minnesota Press, 2004.

Hartmann, Heidi. "The Unhappy Marriage of Marxism and Feminism: Towards a More Progressive Union." *Capital and Class* 3, no. 2 (Summer 1979): 1–33.

Hartsock, Nancy. "The Feminist Standpoint: Developing the Ground for a Specifically Feminist Historical Materialism." In Sandra Harding and Merrill B. Hintikka, *Discovering Reality*, 283–310.

————. "Feminist Theory and Revolutionary Strategy." In Zillah R. Eisenstein, ed. *Capitalist Patriarchy*. New York: Monthly Review Press, 1979, 56–77.

Haug, Frigga. "The Marx within Feminism." In Mojab, *Marxism and Feminism*, 76–101.

Hayden, Dolores. *The Grand Domestic Revolution: A History of Feminist Designs for American Homes, Neighborhoods, and Cities*. Cambridge, MA: MIT Press 1985.

Henninger, Max. "Poverty, Labor, Development: Towards a Critique of Marx's Conceptualizations." In Van der Linden and Roth, *Beyond Marx*, 281–304.

Hewitt, Margaret. *Wives and Mothers in Victorian Industry: A Study of the Effects of the Employment of Married Women in Victorian Industry*. London: Rockliff, 1958.

Himes, Norman Edwin. *Medical History of Contraception*. New York: Schocken Books, 1970 [1936].

Hobsbawm, Eric. *Industry and Empire: The Making of Modern English Society, 1759 to the Present Day*. New York: Pantheon Books, 1968.

Holloway, John. *Change the World without Taking Power: The Meaning of Revolution Today.* London: Pluto Press, 2002.

————. *Crack Capitalism.* London: Pluto Press, 2010.

————. "From Scream of Refusal to Scream of Power: The Centrality of Work." In Bonefeld, Gunn, Holloway, and Psychopedis, *Emancipating Marx,* 155–81.

Holmstrom, Nancy. "A Marxist Theory of Women's Nature." In Holmstrom, *The Socialist Feminist Project,* 360–76.

————, ed. *The Socialist Feminist Project: A Contemporary Reader in Theory and Politics.* New York: Monthly Review Press, 2002.

Holocombe, Lee. *Wives and Property: Reform of the Married Women's Property Law in Nineteenth-Century England.* Toronto: University of Toronto Press, 1983.

Inman, Mary. *In Woman's Defense.* Los Angeles: Committee to Organize the Advancement of Women, 1940.

Jackson, Stevi. "Why a Materialist Feminism Is (Still) Possible." *Women's Studies International Forum* 24, nos. 3–4 (2001): 283–93.

James, Selma. *Sex, Race and Class.* Bristol: Falling Wall Press, 1975.

Kingsnorth, Paul. *One No, Many Yeses: A Journey to the Heart of the Global Resistance Movement.* London: Free Press, 2003.

Klein, Naomi. *This Changes Everything: Capitalism vs. Climate.* New York: Simon and Schuster, 2014.

Kopp, Anatole. *Città e Rivoluzione. Architettura e Urbanistica Sovietiche degli anni Venti.* Edited by E.Battisti. Milano: Feltrinelli, 1972 [1967].

Kovel, Joel. *The Enemy of Nature: The End of Capitalism or the End of the World?* 2nd ed. London: Zed Books, 2007.

————. "On Marx and Ecology." *Capitalism, Nature, Socialism* 22, no. 1 (September 2011): 4–17.

Lenin, V.I. "Two Tactics of Social Democracy in the Democratic Revolution" (1905). In *Selected Works.* Vol. 1. New York: International Publishers, 1971.

Levine Frader, Laura. "Women in the Industrial Capitalist Economy." In Bridenthal, Koonz, and Stuard, *Becoming Visible, Women in European History,* 309–31.

Lopate, Carol. "Women and Pay for Housework." *Liberation* 18, no. 9 (May–June 1974): 8–11.

Lorde, Audre. "The Master's Tools Will Never Dismantle the Master's House." In Moraga and Anzaldua, *This Bridge Called My Back: Writings by Radical Women of Color,* 98–101.

Lown, Judy. *Women and Industrialization: Gender at Work in Nineteenth-Century England.* Minneapolis: University of Minnesota Press, 1990.

Marshall, Alfred. *Principles of Economics: An Introductory Volume.* London: Macmillan and Co., 1938 [1890].

Marx, Karl. "Address of the International Working Men's Association to Abraham Lincoln, President of the United States: Presented to US Ambassador Charles Francis Adams, on January 28, 1985." Accessed April 1, 2021. https://www.marxists.org/archive/marx/iwma/documents/1864/lincoln-letter.htm.

————. *Capital.* Vol. 1. London: Penguin, 1981 [1867].

————. *Capital.* Vol. 3. London: Penguin, 1981 [1885].

————. *A Contribution to the Critique of Political Economy.* Edited by Maurice Dobb. New York: International Publishers, 1970 [1859].

————. *Early Writings.* Edited and translated by T.B. Bottomore. New York: McGraw-Hill Book Company, 1963.

————. *Economic and Philosophical Manuscripts of 1844.* Translated by Martin Milligan. Moscow: Foreign Languages Publishing House, 1961.

————. *The 18th Brumaire of Louis Bonaparte.* New York: International Publishers, 1963 [1852].

————. *Grundrisse: Foundations of the Critique of Political Economy.* London: Pelican Books, 1973.

————. *Theories of Surplus Value, Part 1.* Moscow: Progress Publishers, 1969 [1862–1863].

Marx, Karl, and Frederick Engels. *The Communist Manifesto.* Harmondsworth, UK: Penguin Books, 1967 [1848].

————. *The First Indian War of Independence, 1857–1859.* Moscow: Progress Publishers, 1959 [1911].

————. *The German Ideology*, part 1. New York: International Publishers, 1988 [1932].

Marx-Aveling, Eleanor, and Edward Aveling. *The Woman Question.* Edited by Joachim Muller and Edith Schotte. Leipzig: Verlag fur die Frau, 1986 [1886].

Meillassoux, Claude. *Maidens, Meal and Money: Capitalism and the Domestic Community.* Cambridge: Cambridge University Press, 1975, xi.

Meyer, Ahlrich. "A Theory of Defeat. Marx and the Evidence of the Nineteenth Century." In Van der Linden and Roth, *Beyond Marx*, 258–79.

Mies, Maria. *Patriarchy and Accumulation on a World Scale: Women in the International Division of Labor.* London: Zed Books, 2014 [1985].

Mies, Maria, and Vandana Shiva. *Ecofeminism.* London: Zed Books, 1993.

Mojab, Shahrzad, ed. *Marxism and Feminism.* London: Zed Books, 2015.

Moraga, Cherríe, and Gloria Anzaldua, eds. *This Bridge Called My Back: Writings by Radical Women of Color.* New York: Kitchen Table, 1983.

Morgan, Lewis H. *Ancient Society* (1877). Accessed April 1, 2021. https://www.marxists.org/reference/archive/morgan-lewis/ancient-society/index.htm.

Musto, Marcello. *The Last Years of Karl Marx: An Intellectual Biography.* Palo Alto, CA: Stanford University Press, 2016.

Negri, Antonio. *Marx beyond Marx: Lessons on the Grundrisse.* Edited by Jim Fleming. Translated by Harry Cleaver. Brooklyn: Autonomedia, 1991.

Ollman, Bertell. *Dialectical Investigations.* New York: Routledge, 1993.

Pelz, William A. "Capital and the First International." In Ingo Schmidt and Carlo Fanelli, eds. *Reading "Capital" Today.* London: Pluto Press, 2017.

Pinchbeck, Ivy. *Women Workers and the Industrial Revolution: 1750–1850.* New York: F.S. Crofts & Co, 1930.

Robinson, Cedric. J. *Black Marxism: The Making of the Black Radical Tradition.* Chapel Hill: North Carolina University Press, 1983.

Rosdoldsky, Roman. *The Making of Marx's "Capital."* London: Pluto Press, 1977.

Rosemont, Franklin. "Karl Marx and the Iroquois." In *Arsenal: Surrealist Subversion.* Chicago: Black Swan Press, 1989, 201–13.

Rowbotham, Sheila. *Woman's Consciousness, Man's World.* Baltimore: Penguin Books, 1973.

———. *Women, Resistance, and Revolution.* New York: Vintage Books, 1974.

Sachs, Wolfgang, ed. *The Development Dictionary: A Guide to Knowledge as Power.* London: Zed Books, 1993.

Salleh, Ariel. *Ecofeminism as Politics: Nature, Marx and the Postmodern.* London: Zed Books, 1997.

Sarkar, Saral. *Eco-Socialism or Eco-Capitalism? A Critical Analysis of Humanity's Fundamental Choices.* London: Zed Books, 1999.

Seccombe, Wally. "The Housewife and Her Labour under Capitalism." *New Left Review* no. 83 (January–February 1974): 23.

———. "Patriarchy Stabilized: The Construction of the Male Breadwinner Wage Norm in Nineteenth-Century Britain." *Social History* 11, no. 1 (January 1986): 11, 53–76.

———. *Weathering the Storm: Working-Class Families from the Industrial Revolution to the Fertility Decline.* London: Verso, 1993.

Shanin, Teodor. *Late Marx and the Russian Road: Marx and the "Peripheries" of Capitalism.* New York: Monthly Review Press, 1983.

Taylor, Barbara. "The Men Are as Bad as Their Masters . . .': Socialism, Feminism, and Sexual Antagonism in the London Tailoring Trade in the Early 1830s," *Feminist Studies* 5, no. 1 (Spring 1979): 7–40.

Thompson, E.P. *Customs in Common: Studies in Traditional Popular Culture.* New York: New Press, 1991.

Thurton, Roderick. "Marxism in the Caribbean." In *Two Lectures by Roderick Thurton: A Second Memorial Pamphlet.* New York: George Caffentzis and Silvia Federici, 2000.

Tomasello, Federico. *L'Inizio del lavoro: Teoria politica e questione sociale nella Francia di prima metá Ottocento.* Roma: Carrocci Editore, 2018.

Ulrich, Otto. "Technology." In Wolfgang Sachs, *The Development Dictionary*, 275–87.

United Nations Population Fund. *State of the World Population 2001.* New York: United Nations, 2001.

Van der Linden, Marcel, and Karl Heinz Roth, eds. *Beyond Marx: Theorizing the Global Labor Relations of the Twentieth-First Century.* Leiden, NL: Brill, 2014.

Vercellone, Carlo. "From Formal Subsumption to General Intellect: Elements for a Marxist Reading of the Thesis of Cognitive Capitalism." *Historical Materialism* 15, no. 1 (2007): 13–36.

Vogel, Lisa. "The Earthly Family." *Radical America* 7, nos. 4–5 (July–October 1973).

Wallach Scott, Joan. *Gender and the Politics of History.* New York: Columbia University Press, 1988.

Weatherford, Jack. *Indian Givers: How the Indians of the Americas Transformed the World.* New York: Fawcett Books, 1988.

Weigand, Kate. *Red Feminism: American Communism and the Making of Women's Liberation.* Baltimore: Johns Hopkins University Press, 2001.

Workers Fight no. 79 (December 1974–January 1975).

Worldwatch Institute. "State of the World 2011: Innovations That Nourish the Planet" (press release), June 16, 2014. Accessed April 2, 2021. http://www.environmentandsociety.org/mml/state-world-2011-innovations-nourish-planet.

Zaretsky, Eli. "Socialist Politics and the Family." *Socialist Revolution* 3, no. 19 (January–March 1974).

Index

"Passim" (literally "scattered") indicates intermittent discussion of a topic over a cluster of pages.

About the Author

Silvia Federici is a feminist writer, teacher, and militant. In 1972, she was cofounder of the International Feminist Collective, which launched the Wages for Housework campaign. Her books include: *Caliban and the Witch*; *Re-enchanting the World*; and *Witches, Witch-Hunting, and Women*. She is a professor emerita at Hofstra University, where she taught social sciences. She worked as a teacher in Nigeria and was also the cofounder of the Committee for Academic Freedom in Africa.

ABOUT PM PRESS

PM Press is an independent, radical publisher
of books and media to educate, entertain, and
inspire. Founded in 2007 by a small group of
people with decades of publishing, media, and
organizing experience, PM Press amplifies the
voices of radical authors, artists, and activists.

Our aim is to deliver bold political ideas and vital stories to all walks
of life and arm the dreamers to demand the impossible. We have sold
millions of copies of our books, most often one at a time, face to face.
We're old enough to know what we're doing and young enough to know
what's at stake. Join us to create a better world.

PM Press
PO Box 23912
Oakland, CA 94623
www.pmpress.org

PM Press in Europe
europe@pmpress.org
www.pmpress.org.uk

FRIENDS OF PM PRESS

These are indisputably momentous times—the financial system is melting down globally and the Empire is stumbling. Now more than ever there is a vital need for radical ideas.

In the years since its founding—and on a mere shoestring—PM Press has risen to the formidable challenge of publishing and distributing knowledge and entertainment for the struggles ahead. With over 450 releases to date, we have published an impressive and stimulating array of literature, art, music, politics, and culture. Using every available medium, we've succeeded in connecting those hungry for ideas and information to those putting them into practice.

Friends of PM allows you to directly help impact, amplify, and revitalize the discourse and actions of radical writers, filmmakers, and artists. It provides us with a stable foundation from which we can build upon our early successes and provides a much-needed subsidy for the materials that can't necessarily pay their own way. You can help make that happen—and receive every new title automatically delivered to your door once a month—by joining as a Friend of PM Press. And, we'll throw in a free T-shirt when you sign up.

Here are your options:

- **$30 a month** Get all books and pamphlets plus 50% discount on all webstore purchases

- **$40 a month** Get all PM Press releases (including CDs and DVDs) plus 50% discount on all webstore purchases

- **$100 a month** Superstar—Everything plus PM merchandise, free downloads, and 50% discount on all webstore purchases

For those who can't afford $30 or more a month, we have **Sustainer Rates** at $15, $10 and $5. Sustainers get a free PM Press T-shirt and a 50% discount on all purchases from our website.

Your Visa or Mastercard will be billed once a month, until you tell us to stop. Or until our efforts succeed in bringing the revolution around. Or the financial meltdown of Capital makes plastic redundant. Whichever comes first.

Revolution at Point Zero
Housework, Reproduction, and Feminist Struggle, Second Edition

Silvia Federici

ISBN: 978-1-62963-797-6
$17.95   256 pages

Written between 1974 and 2012, *Revolution at Point Zero* collects forty years of research and theorizing on the nature of housework, social reproduction, and women's struggles on this terrain—to escape it, to better its conditions, to reconstruct it in ways that provide an alternative to capitalist relations.

Indeed, as Federici reveals, behind the capitalist organization of work and the contradictions inherent in "alienated labor" is an explosive ground zero for revolutionary practice upon which are decided the daily realities of our collective reproduction.

Beginning with Federici's organizational work in the Wages for Housework movement, the essays collected here unravel the power and politics of wide but related issues including the international restructuring of reproductive work and its effects on the sexual division of labor, the globalization of care work and sex work, the crisis of elder care, the development of affective labor, and the politics of the commons.

This new and expanded edition contains two previously unpublished essays by the author.

"Federici has become a crucial figure for young Marxists, political theorists, and a new generation of feminists."
—Rachel Kushner author of *The Flamethrowers*

"Federici's attempt to draw together the work of feminists and activist from different parts of the world and place them in historical context is brave, thought-provoking and timely. Federici's writing is lucid and her fury palpable."
—Red Pepper

Re-enchanting the World: Feminism and the Politics of the Commons

Silvia Federici
with a Foreword by Peter Linebaugh

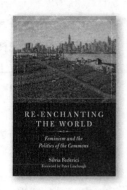

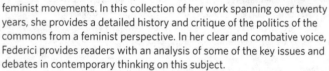

ISBN: 978-1-62963-569-9
$19.95   240 pages

Silvia Federici is one of the most important
contemporary theorists of capitalism and
feminist movements. In this collection of her work spanning over twenty
years, she provides a detailed history and critique of the politics of the
commons from a feminist perspective. In her clear and combative voice,
Federici provides readers with an analysis of some of the key issues and
debates in contemporary thinking on this subject.

Drawing on rich historical research, she maps the connections
between the previous forms of enclosure that occurred with the
birth of capitalism and the destruction of the commons and the "new
enclosures" at the heart of the present phase of global capitalist
accumulation. Considering the commons from a feminist perspective,
this collection centers on women and reproductive work as crucial to
both our economic survival and the construction of a world free from
the hierarchies and divisions capital has planted in the body of the world
proletariat. Federici is clear that the commons should not be understood
as happy islands in a sea of exploitative relations but rather autonomous
spaces from which to challenge the existing capitalist organization of life
and labor.

*"Silvia Federici's theoretical capacity to articulate the plurality that fuels the
contemporary movement of women in struggle provides a true toolbox for
building bridges between different features and different people."*
—Massimo De Angelis, professor of political economy, University of
East London

*"Silvia Federici's work embodies an energy that urges us to rejuvenate
struggles against all types of exploitation and, precisely for that reason, her
work produces a common: a common sense of the dissidence that creates a
community in struggle."*
—Maria Mies, coauthor of *Ecofeminism*